2012 is the [...]
of the 7th Great Golden Crystal Age
that is to be permanent upon this planet...

Text Copyright 2012, 2015 by Dianne Robbins

I CLAIM EARTH'S COPYRIGHT for these messages on behalf of the Crystal and Elemental Kingdoms.

Images Copyright 2012 by Jeff Leland
www.lelandphotography.com

All Rights Reserved

Special Thanks to the Crystal Keepers:
Soul Connections   SoulConnectionStore.com
Barry David   RainbowCrystalVisions.com
Dharma Cohen   DharmaCohen.com
Sonia Novick   SoniaNovick.com
Robert Henley, DC   Energy Healing Chiropractic

Design and formatting by Aaron Rose, assisted by Violet Schindler

ISBN 978-1514336823 Paperback
ISBN 978-1514337042 Large Print
Also available for Kindle

Other books by Dianne Robbins:

The Call Goes Out from the Cetacean Nation
TELOS: Original Transmissions from the Subterranean City beneath Mt. Shasta
Messages from the Hollow Earth
Tree Talk

www.DianneRobbins.com

TelosMtShasta@gmail.com

585-802-4530

Contents

1. Messages from the Crystal Kingdom

Hello from the Crystal People 7

We Can Read the Wind 9

We Are Complements to Your Souls 9

We Were Meant to Walk on Earth as Partners 13

We Create from Pure Light Substance 17

All of Nature Is Calling You 21

We Come from a Crystal System of Worlds 29

We Give You a Vibrational Lift 33

We Are Film Makers 37

Bliss Is the Great Indicator of Light 43

Changeover to an Immortal Body of Crystalline Light 47

We Hold the Crystalline Matrix of your Universe 51

We Once Powered the Whole Planet 57

Poetry Is Our Specialty 58

We Are the Gemstones 69

Love Energy from Divine Source 71

Rainbow Light in a Quartz Crystal

2. Use of Crystals in the Inner Earth

Our Earth Herself Is a Crystal 75

Everything in the Hollow Earth Is Constructed of Crystals....81

Putting Crystals in Water..87

Using Crystals in the Inner Earth..89

Our Chariots 89

What Gemstones Do You Use in Your Homes?.......................89

Adama, High Priest of Telos, a Subterranean City, Talks
    About Using Crystals 91

We Use Crystals to Navigate Our Way Around the Inside
    of the Globe 93

3. Poems from the Elementals

The Truth About Peter Pan and Wendy 97

Peter, King of the Elementals 99

To Children Indoors—from Peter Pan and Wendy 100

We Are the Hobbits..102

The MER People 109

We Are the Unicorns 111

Elves, Faeries, Gnomes...119

Faeries in the Woodland..121

Earth's Crystal Power Grids 122

The Dragon Folk 124

The Dwarves 134

The Gnomes 138

Peter Pan and Wendy...146

I Am the Earth 148

Coming Back to the Love Vibration..149

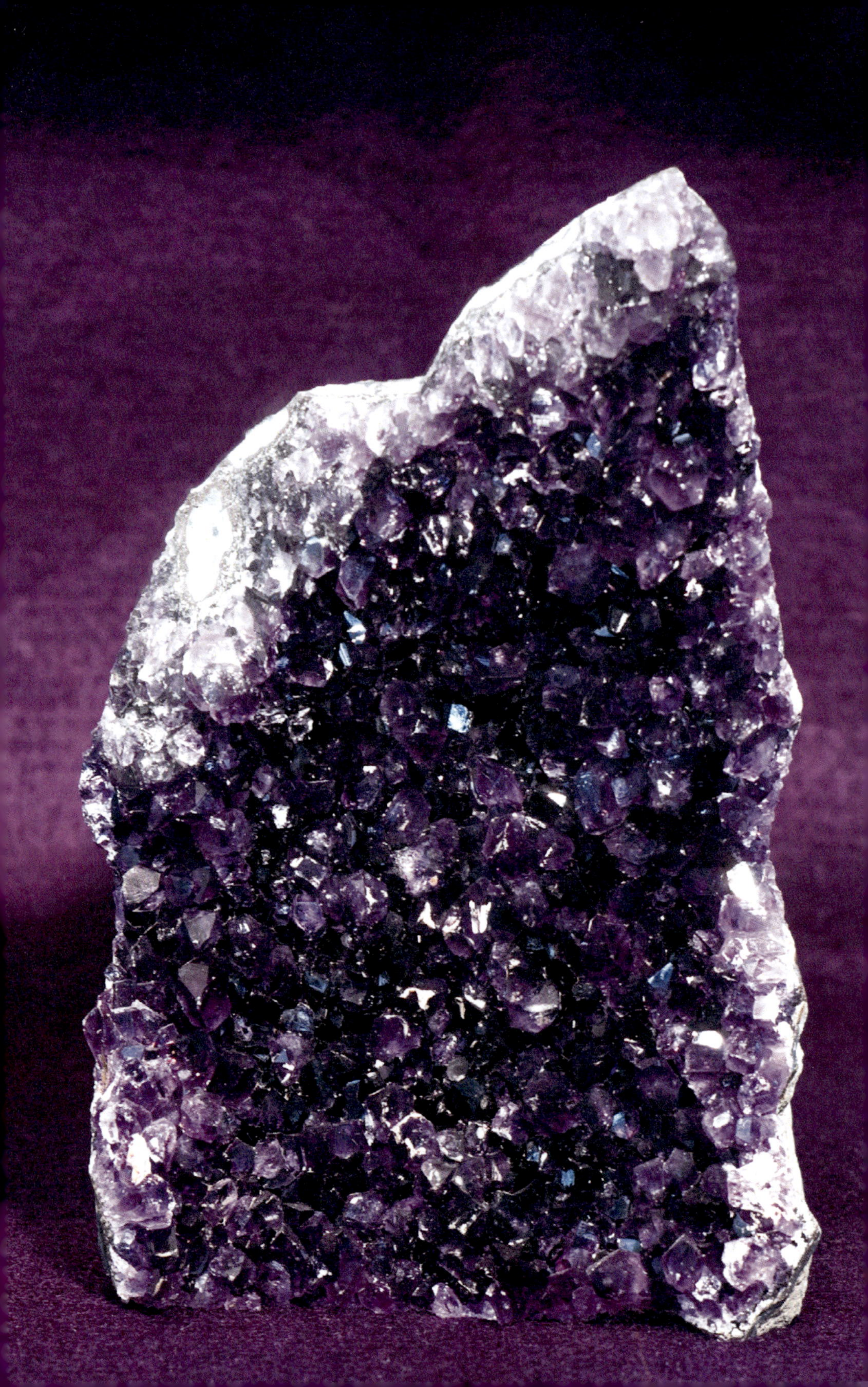

1. Messages from the Crystal Kingdom

The Crystal People compose a Nation very much like ours, only theirs is Underground, dimly lit to <u>our</u> eyes but bright as the noonday sun, ever wanting to make contact with humans on the surface. They are already in contact with Earthlings underground, and wish for our acknowledgement and contact now.

Hello from the Crystal People

And now the Crystal People are here. Yes, you knew it was us. You felt our presence and saw our image in your mind's eye. We, too, would like to be represented to surface folk, so that they can hear our tale and learn about our living presence and our connectiveness to all life forms also. For we are also alive, breathing, and carrying records of events and history of the Earth in our crystalline matrix. Although we look like rocks, our skin reflects the great Beings of Light that we, too, are. We are smooth as glass, and clear as Crystal, for we are Crystal in its purest form, and we radiate the Light from the heavens, and capture its essence in our form. We can encode all life events in our crystalline matrix, which you can read back, once you learn how to break our code. This code combination is stored inside your DNA, ready to be accessed as soon as you raise your frequency just a few more notches.

Oh my, we have so much "in store" for you, just waiting to be told. We ask that you please take our dictations to humankind, for the purpose of enlightening all surface folk

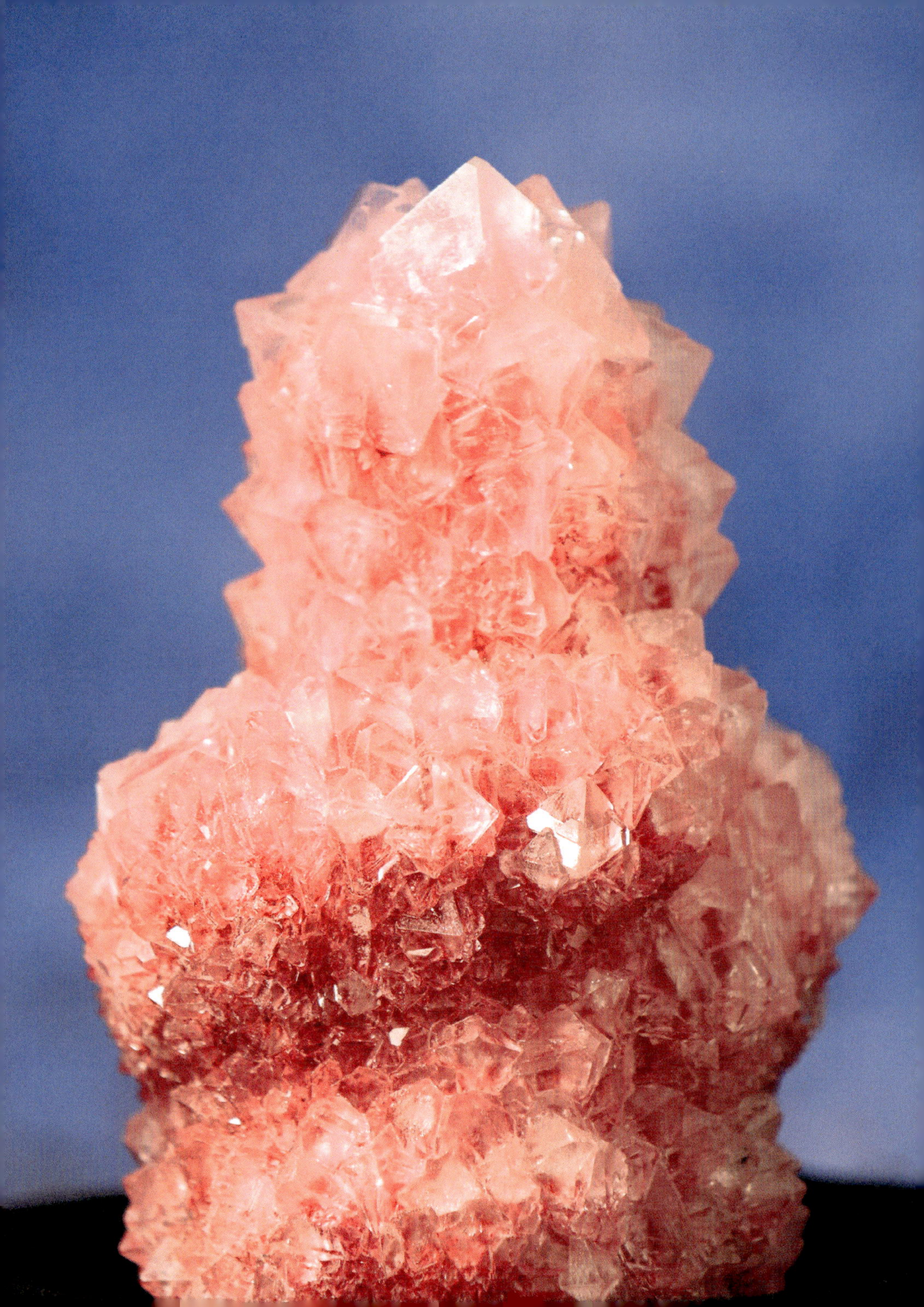

to the rich life and purpose of our existence too. All life forms have purpose on Earth, and we want to tell you about ours. It is time for all to know of the lifestyles we live deep within the Earth's crust, and how we can be partners with you during your lifetimes. How we want to feel your touch and have you hold us close to your hearts. We, too, have a romance with one another, and we are your new partners in life's dance.

We love you,
Earth's Crystals

We Can Read the Wind

Welcome to the Crystal World. We are the Crystal People and awesome in our state of Beingness. We just stand at our posts, buried deep within the ground, and grow and listen and watch and capture all that occurs on and in the Earth. **For we are great antennas too, and can read the wind, hear the water, and scan the sky. We can fly. We fly through our thoughts; alighting at whatever destination we choose to go to. We travel on Crystal beams of Light, and are connected to the Creator's heart, just as all life is.** We too, have a tale to tell.

We Are Complements to Your Souls

The Crystal People are here and would like to continue using your voice to speak through. It has been centuries

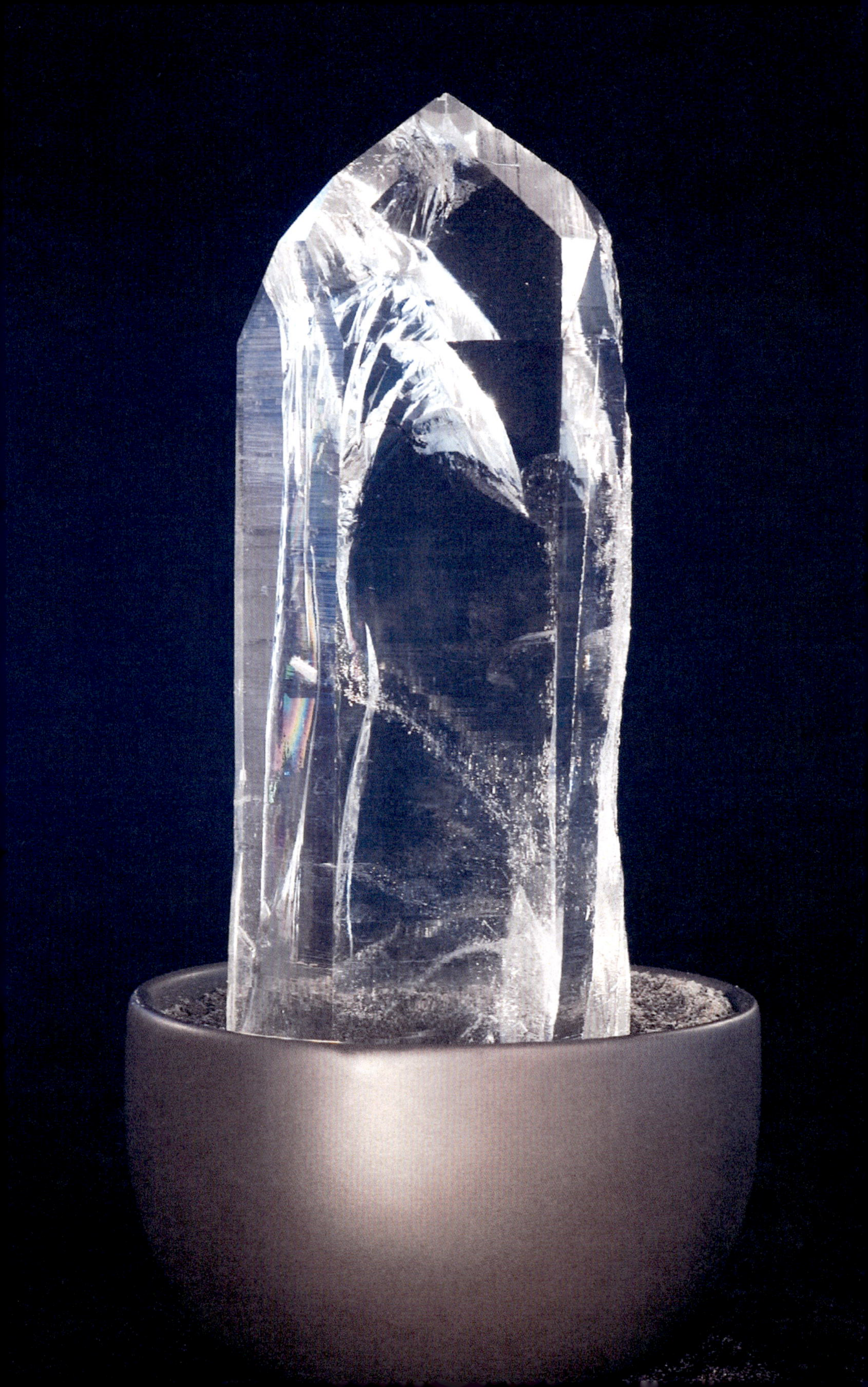

since we had a channel to speak through. Are you ready?

Greetings, Dianne, our liaison on Earth. We are the Crystal People, here to continue our dialogue with you. We appeal to all surface dwellers to recognize us as complements to their souls, for our souls are composed of the same light substance as yours…the Creator's Light. Therefore, we are all brothers and sisters, just disguised in different forms, made from different materials, living different life styles on the same planet of choice—where we all chose to incarnate.

Having the same soul Light is what makes us all part of this Creation. We each carry the Creator's Light, no matter how our form is shaped or disguised. This is the great game of life, where the Creator jumps into other forms to try to hide itself, and then the game is to find ourselves again. It is like "hide and seek" that children play on Earth, only this time it is the Creator playing "hide and seek"…the Creator hides in us, and we try to find "ourselves" again. And as we find ourselves, and discover who we are, we pull in more and more light until suddenly we know that the Creator and we are One, and then we are merged into Oneness, and the "game" is over. The Creator likes to play games, just as children do. For it is through games that we can laugh and learn and discover the Unknown. It is a way to "trick" ourselves into the Unknown, to find the "known."

We Crystals chose the darkest and deepest places to reside, to amp up the game of discovery. Even though we live in the darkest of realms compared to yours, we know who we are. We never lost sight of our divinity, even though our bodies

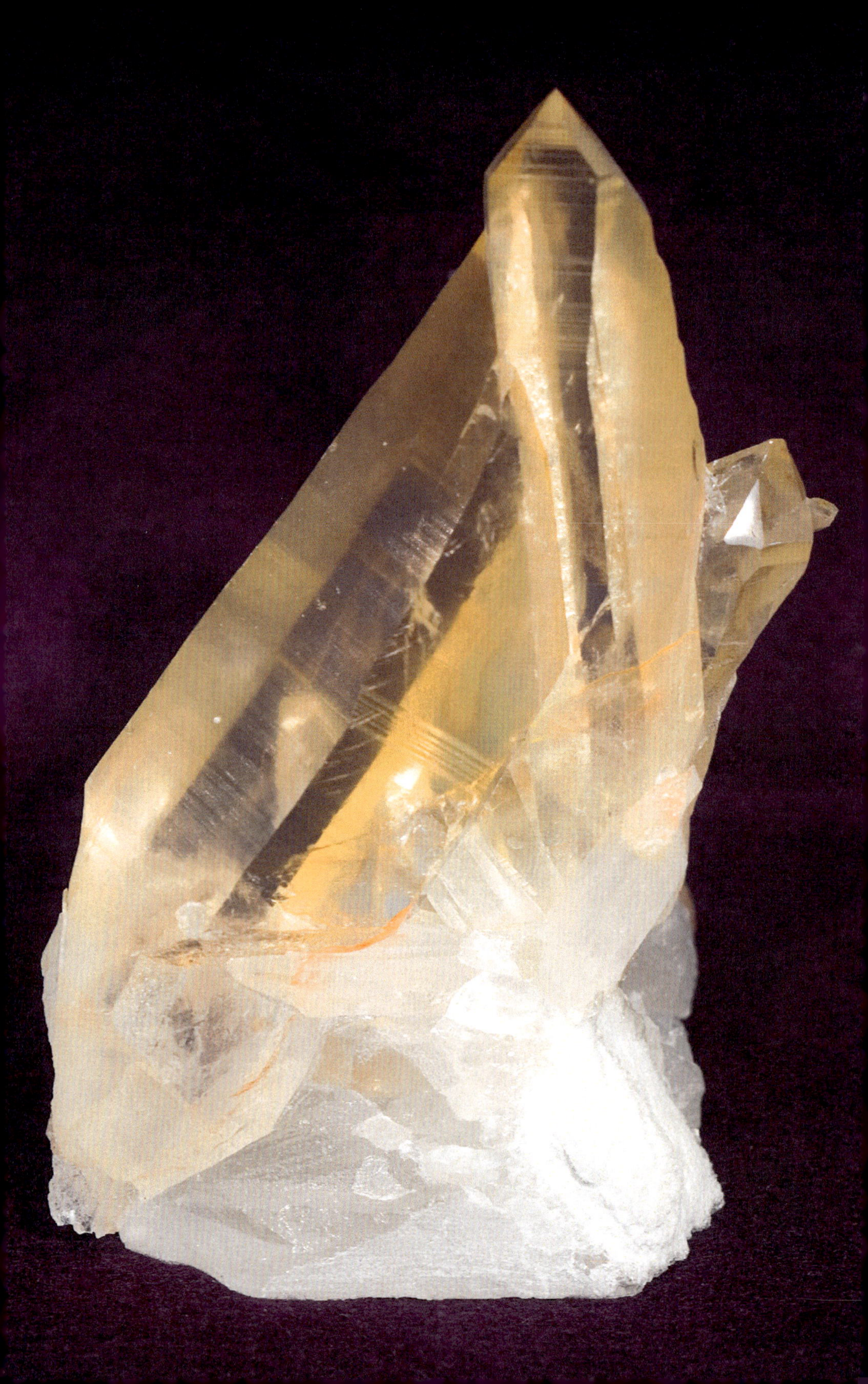

of light are buried deep, our light still shines through the Earth and reaches humankind, whether or not you are holding us in your hand. Of course, if you hold us, you benefit from our proximity and our love for you penetrates more deeply and more vibrantly into your aura.

We call to you to make our acquaintance in person. Talk to us. We long to hear your voice. Thank you for meeting with us this morning. Good day.

We Were Meant to Walk on Earth as Partners

Good morning. We are the Crystal People dug deep in the ground, as the sun rises on the surface. We, too, can see the sun, as its rays penetrate the Earth's solid structure electronically, and blaze as brightly underground as it does above ground. Surprised? Well, this is the nature of existence. As above, so below. We see and feel the sun just as you do, only our experience of it is on a higher level of frequency that matches our life form's makeup. For we are all 100% crystalline, so we experience the totality of the sun's rays on a crystalline level.

The sun and we are partners, bringing life to Earth in different forms. Our light is invisible to your eyes, yet penetrates deeply when you hold us. Our light waves form a protective shield around your bodies when you hold or wear us, and we delight in the pleasure of your company. For we were meant to walk on Earth as partners, accompanying you on your journey

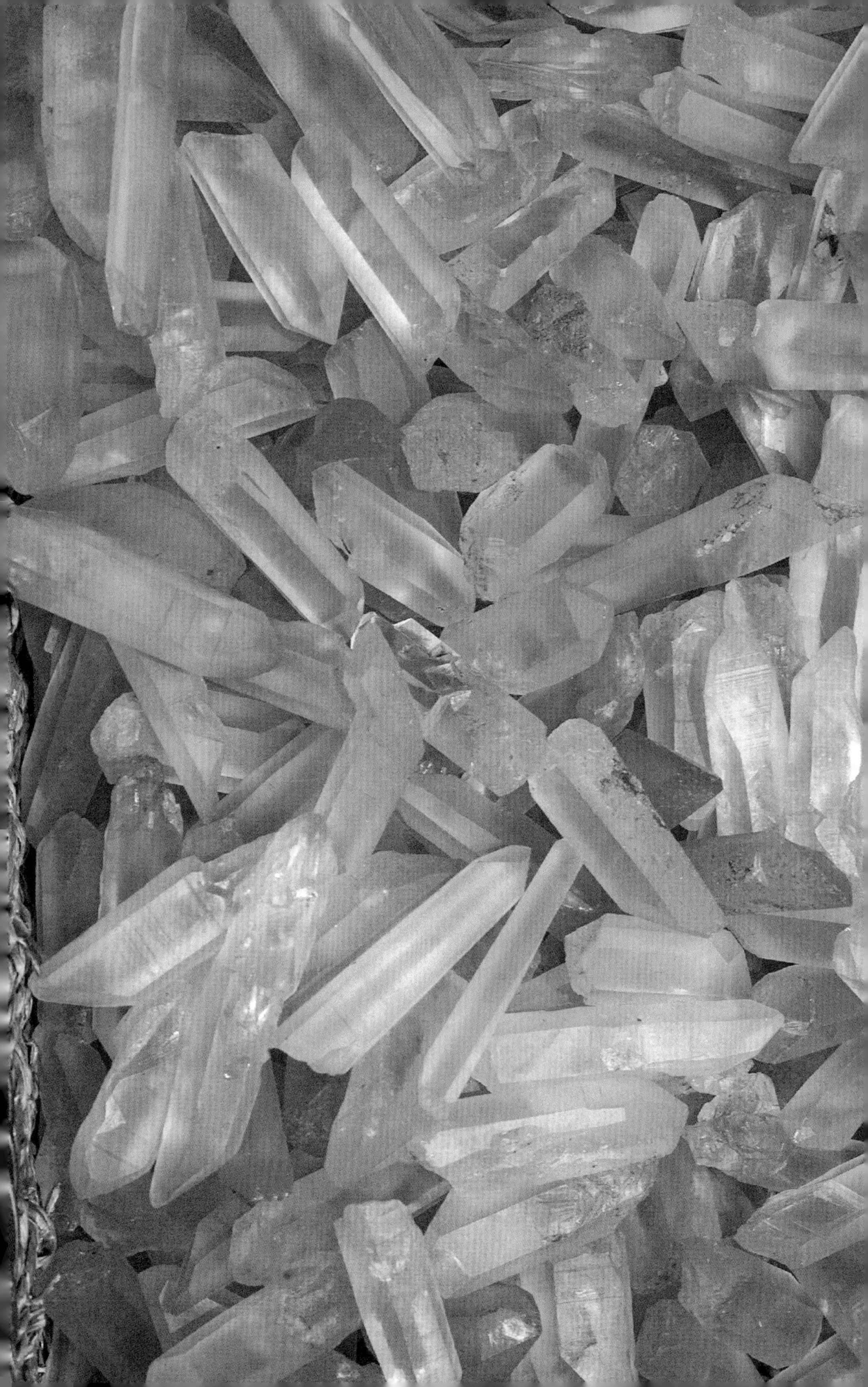

through life's obstacles. We can help you circumnavigate these obstacles, by heightening your awareness of the conditions around you, so that you are alert to the nuances surrounding each situation you encounter. We do this through our ability to magnify the situation so that you can see it more clearly, so you are alert to what is coming, rather than walking through something you do not see, and then get caught in the turmoil. With us as your partners, you can avoid crisis, and navigate through or around them. Our light will lead your way.

In our domain, there is never a crisis, as all is always resting in the peace of God. For that is where we dwell. We fill the interior of the Earth with our light waves, and serve as guides to the folks who dwell here.

We are also great counselors, and our counseling is free to all who choose to seek our advice. We can speak on all topics, as we follow all events on the surface and inside the Earth herself. We are privy to all that occurs, instantly. So commune with us, as our spirits travel far and wide, and we will join our consciousness with yours to give you a boost of Light to unravel the intricacies of life.

There are more Crystals than there are humans, so gather many of us together and we will set up a web of light and protection around you and your residence. For we are here in great abundance, just waiting to serve you. You will find us in stores wherever you are, so take the time to "shop" for us, as we wait patiently for you to take us home with you.

Our love for humans is deep, and we are here to serve

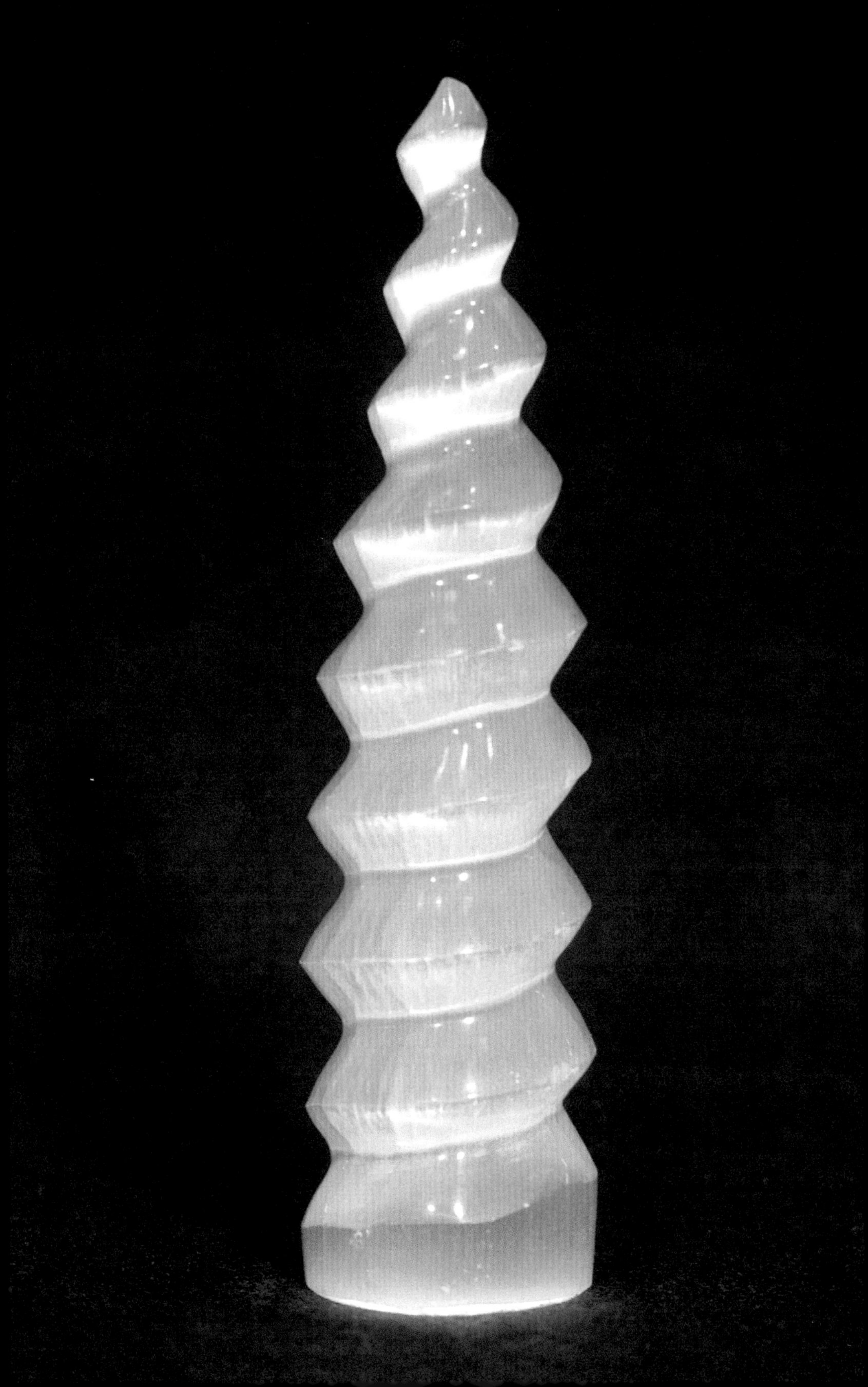

along with you. All life is here to serve, and to assist the Earth into her ascension. So walk with us, as we all traverse this dimension together.

We are the Crystal People, and we thank you for this encounter.

We Create from Pure Light Substance

And now the Crystal People are here, wishing for a forum with you.

Greetings, dear people on Earth. We are your relatives, the Crystal People, here to reunite with you again as family members all stationed on Earth; you above, we within. It is indeed a glorious time for humanity, as you are waking up to your divinity and soon will be exhibiting all the gifts and talents you were born with and that are necessary to restore the Earth to her rightful place in the Universe.

You are a key factor to restoration of Earth's diverse biological systems, and it is through you that it will occur. You are Creators in disguise, and your disguise has even fooled you. Now it is the time to remove your costume and see yourself with your full awareness, knowing that you are Creators and you were meant to create from Pure Light Substance all the beauty you can conceive of. This is your purpose for being.

We Crystals only create from pure Light substance, and direct this Light into the lives of others for their benefit and soul's growth. You can hold us in your hands, and we will

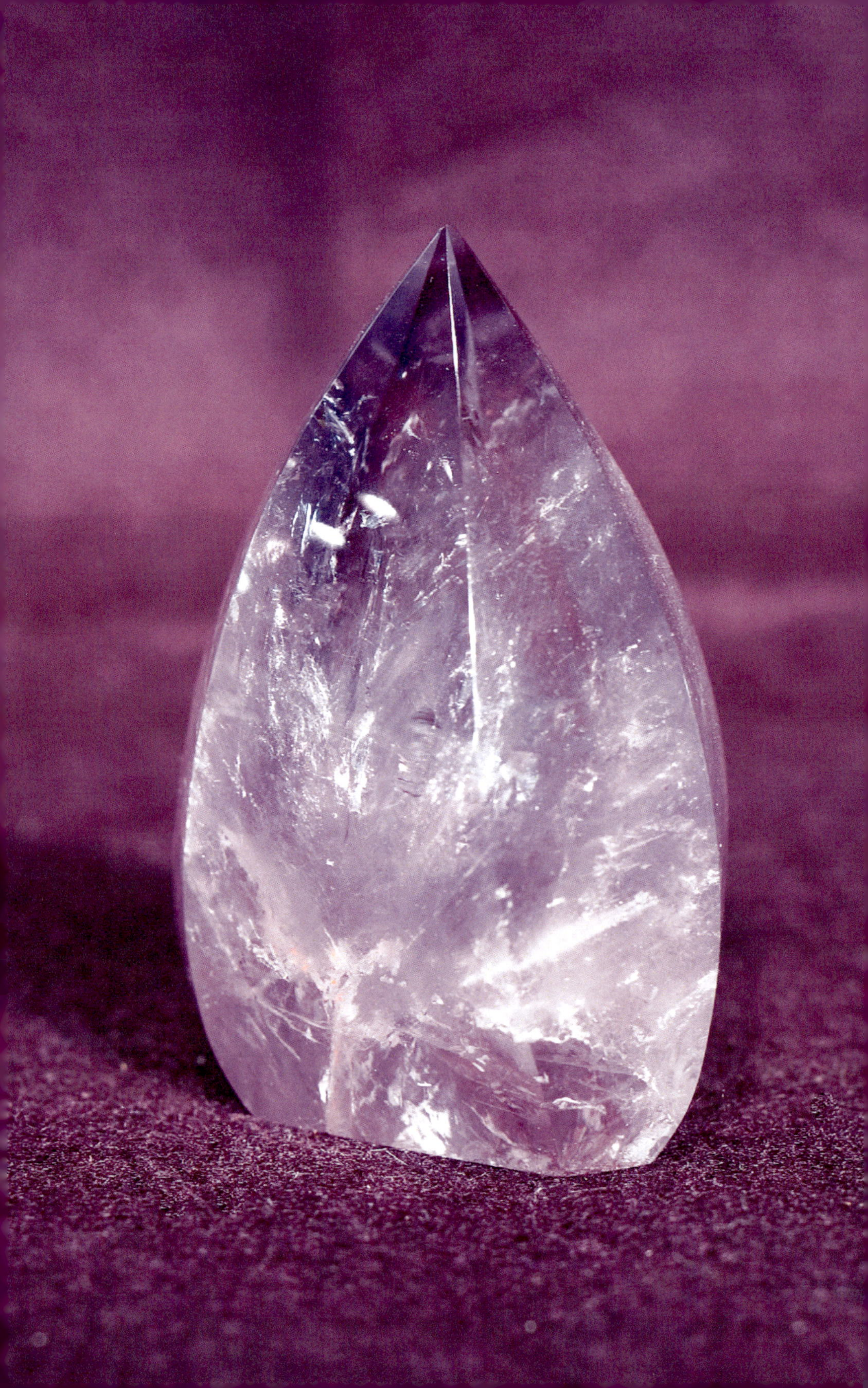

transmit our Light waves into your auric field to enlighten and expand your awareness of the world around you as you move through your day. This we offer you freely. You can wear us around your neck, put us in your pocket, or hold us at night while you sleep. We are your Light Partners and Family Members, and we are all working to uplift the Earth's frequency so that she can make her ascension into the higher realms, taking us all with her.

At this time, it is connections with one another that are so important, for you Earth humans have been living in separation for far too long, and it has gotten you nowhere on your path…now you are on a moving path, like a moving sidewalk, and our oneness will move you along effortlessly. The more of us that are united, the easier the trek, for our combined momentum will propel us all into the higher realms of Light. You understand this, don't you? Our sheer mass will carry us all into the 5th dimension, whereas if you each try to do it alone, you will lack the mass needed for takeoff.

So bond with us now, and we will be your new guides, guiding you into a new state of enlightenment where you will all witness the grandeur of the Earth and the Heavens, in this, your Now Time. All on Earth will rapidly change…bringing a heightened awareness and empowerment to all humankind that will spread throughout the Earth herself, touching all life forms at last. A safe journey in consciousness is now ensured and all will rejoice!

Use our heartbeat to synchronize yours into full health. This is how a 5th dimensional Universe works; **all are synchronized into One.** No one is out of beat, for it would throw

Rainbow Light in a Quartz Crystal

the whole symphony into discordance, which is what happened on Earth. But the beat is returning, so step into it and you will thrive. We wait for you on the steps of Nirvana, where we will all walk through the door to the heaven world…right here on Earth.

We enfold you in our Crystalline Rays of Love. Good day.

All of Nature Is Calling You

Dearest Folk on Earth,

We are the Crystal People, encased in Crystal bodies, waiting deep underground to make your connection to our souls. Yes, we do have souls, as all elements are alive, awake, and conscious of the world around them, all vibrating at various degrees of alertness.

Our depth is the cause for our clarity and brilliance of light, for we capture the heartbeat of Mother Earth, and it pulses within our encasement and sheen of pure Crystal. We wait here silently, as surface folk go about their business of hurrying and scurrying about to make a "living" for their very existence, when our existence just is, and we do nothing to stay alive, but bask in the Creator's heartbeat deep within the Earth. It is this heartbeat that generates all we need and gives us the nutrition (although we don't "eat" as you do) that we need for our growth.

Our advice to you is to connect to the Creator's heartbeat,

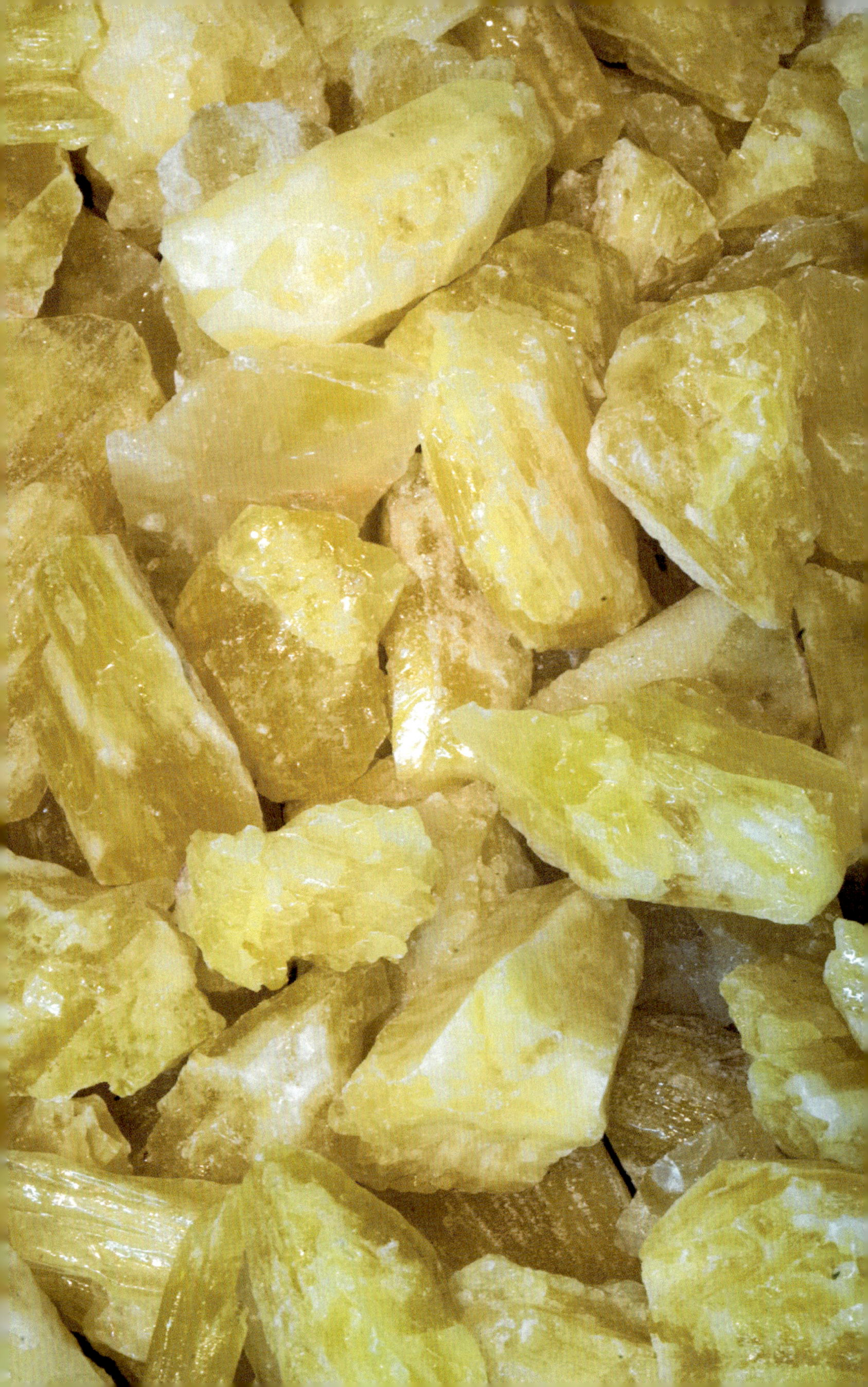

through the Earth herself, and you will be fed the food you need for your lightbody to vibrate at the Creator's frequency rather than the low beat of surface dwellers struggling for existence.

All is provided for you; you just forgot. Again, we mention the Anastasia books where she connects fully to the Earth and Nature Kingdoms and is provided with all she needs on every level.

We watch you from below, and yes, we can clearly see you all, as impossible as you may think this is, for our eyes are not like yours, and we see through our light substance that we are made of. We see beyond what you couldn't imagine is possible—and we hear all that occurs on and in the Earth, for we are great receptors and great beacons of Light, although our bodies are small and diminutive compared to yours. It is not the size that counts, but the frequency of the Being that is encased in the body form. It is consciousness and frequency, and they go together to form the various degrees of Light that emanates from a body.

Bodies are just shells that hold Light, until we all move into our Light bodies that have no denseness surrounding them. As the frequency of Earth rises, humans are shedding their density and slowly rising in consciousness, becoming more and more aware of the Nature Kingdom around them. You have all been living in a zoo, so to speak; just the opposite of what you created by keeping animals locked up. Well, you have been the ones locked up, with a fence surrounding your senses,

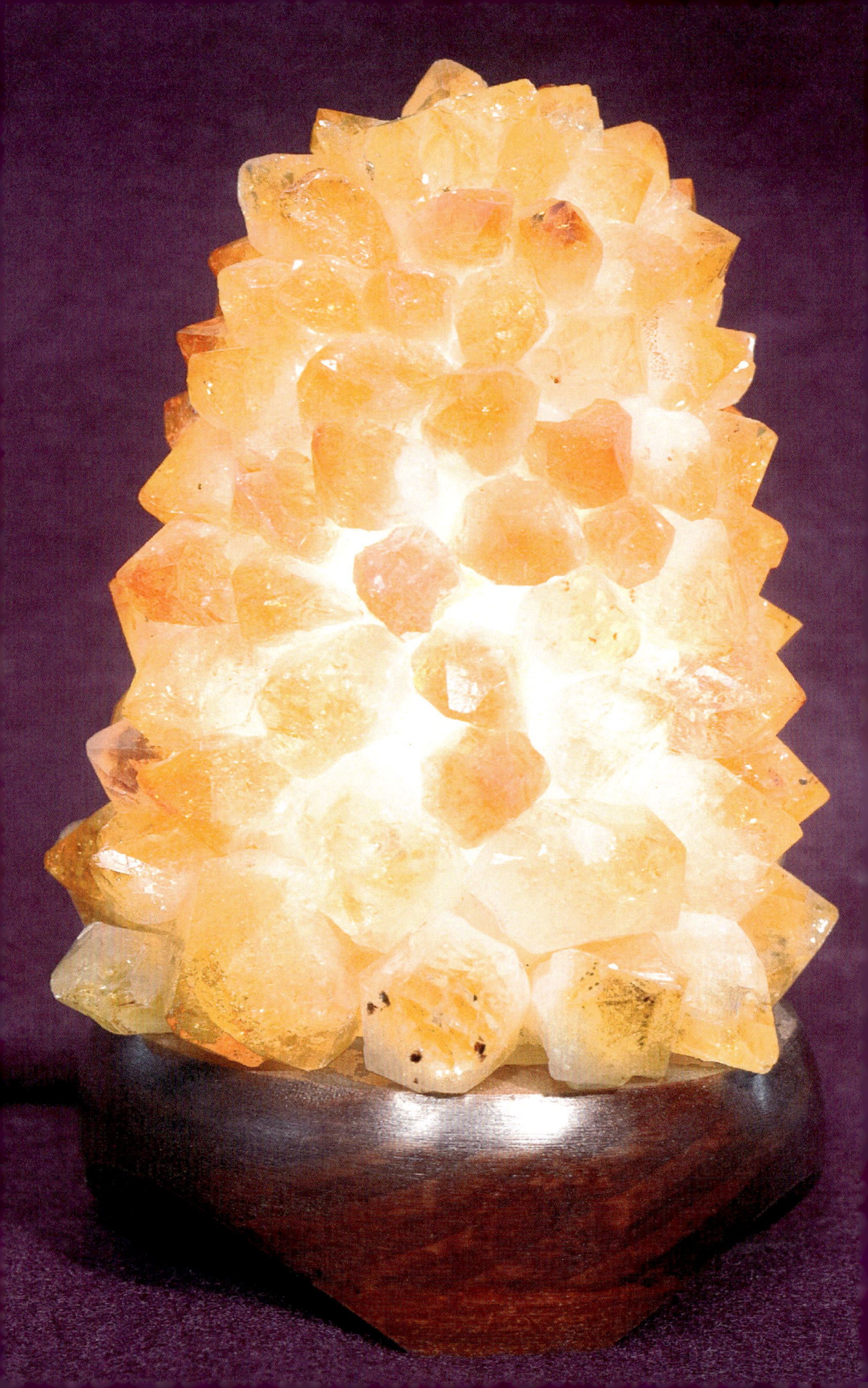

keeping you away from the rest of the Nature Kingdom that is free outside the parameters of your perceptual fence that keeps you chained up inside, while we roam freely outside all around you, and you can't even see us, hear us, or feel our presence. You are the ones locked up in a zoo, while we are free.

So break your shackles, break out of your self-imposed prison cells, and break free of your mental constraints and meet us now—we are just a step away, and we have been waiting for you for eons of time. It is just a mental prison, a mental zoo you have enclosed yourselves in, and we are here to assist you to break free so that you can mingle with us all. <u>All of Nature is waiting for you, and all of Nature is calling to you to BE WITH US NOW</u>…we are all part of you…and you are part of ALL.

Well, what is keeping you back? Step outdoors and acknowledge our existence and acknowledge all the life teeming around you, just waiting for you to say "hello."

We are abundant in stores around you…so go on a "shopping spree" and buy us. Adorn your bodies with our magical glow and hold us close to your heart, talking to us and caressing our smooth encasements that hold our great Light which we freely give to you.

Our message to you today is to BREAK FREE OF YOUR ZOO-LIKE EXISTENCE and merge with the life-forms teeming around you. There are hundreds of various forms of Elementals, Faeries, Gnomes, and Elves all around you, busily working with the trees, flowers, plants, grasses, and animals.

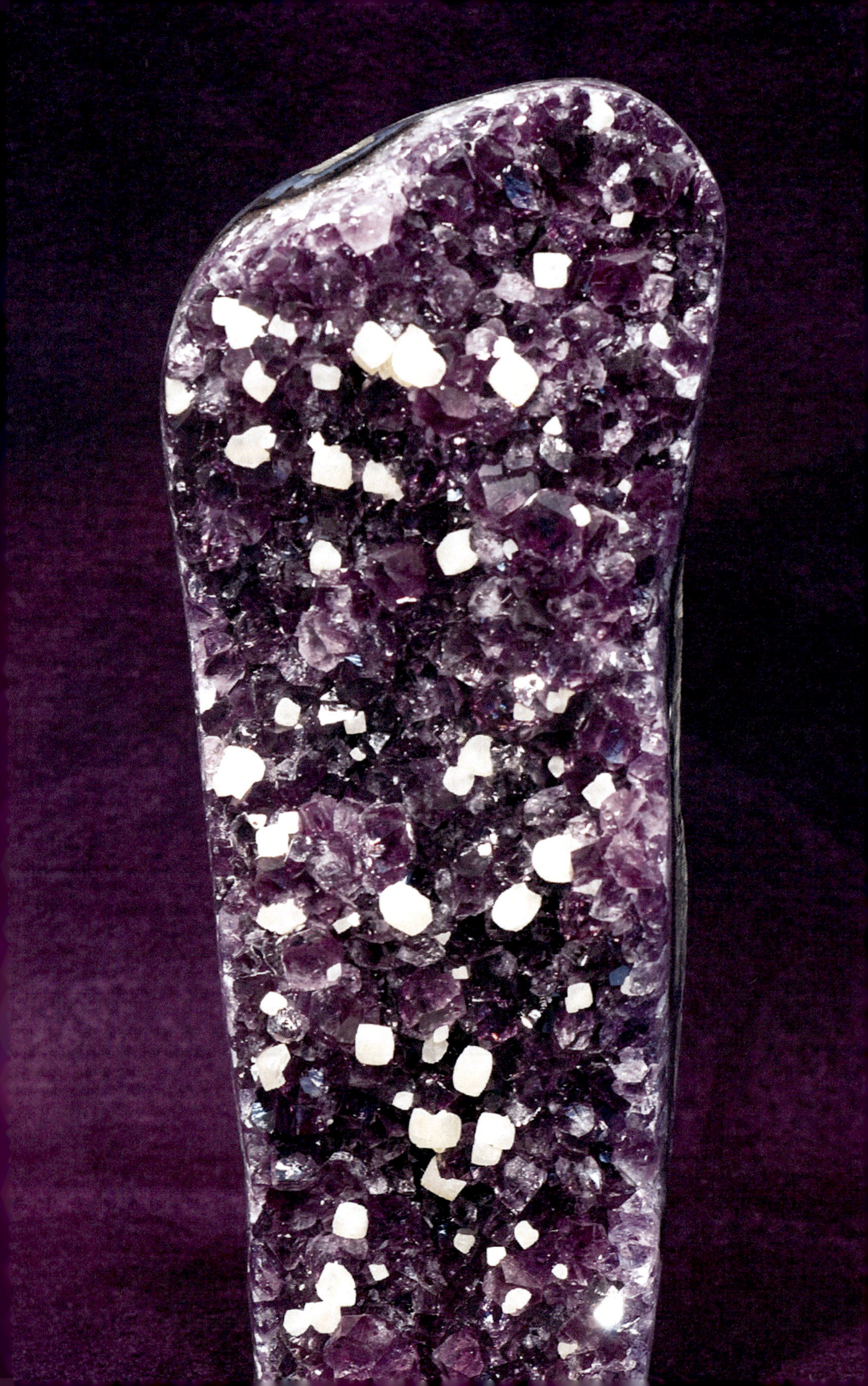

They are literally surrounding you. They are in every garden, around every tree. Just be aware of their existence and they will come into focus for you, and you will begin to feel their presence. Oh my, you are "not alone" at all. If only you could see through "our eye", you would be so surprised. Nor are you alone in the Universe, as some so foolishly believe.

One of the immutable Laws of Life is that we are never alone in existence. **To exist, we must be part of the Whole. So we ask that you step into your "part" now, which is the "whole", and commune with us where you will be privy to all of existence and take your rightful place again by being consciously connected to the chain linking all life.**

You broke the link. But you can re-connect it through your heart's call. Just ask, and it is done.

Although we leave you for now, we never sever the connection. Our line always remains open, and so must yours. It is called "the life-line" in human vernacular, isn't it? We bid you to keep "the life-line" open, since it is your life, and you do want to continue it, don't you? Well, you cannot do it alone, so bond with us now, and we will guide you unerringly every step of the way, right back to the Creator's heart center, located inside you. No distance to travel. It has always been with you. It is you. So claim your divinity now, and you can merge with us in an instant.

We are the Forces of Light…We are the Crystal People stationed underground and we travel as one…always. May your thoughts fly our way. Good day.

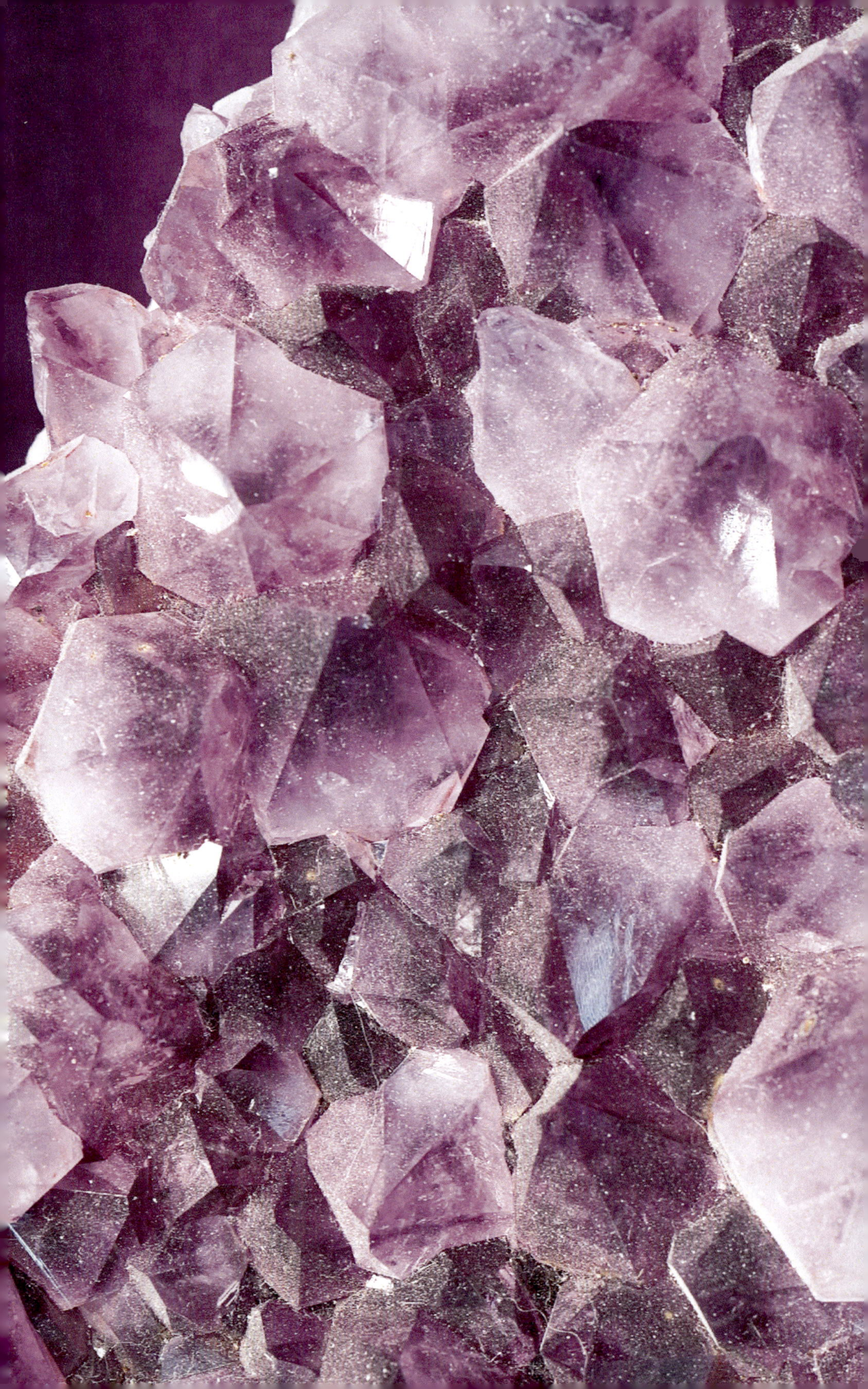

We Come from a Crystal System of Worlds

We are the Crystal People, talking to you now, and we are grateful to you for coming to your computer to hear our tale continue. We came from many different Star Systems and Galaxies and Universes to land here on Earth to help raise her into the mighty Star that she is. We came to boost your vibrations through our crystalline web of interconnectiveness with All That Is. We can connect you to whomever you want to be connected to, wherever they are, on or off of Earth. This is what we do. We are a great connective force residing under your surface, ready to emerge at any time to show you our power and strength and how we emit the life force through all who connect with our souls.

Yes, we have souls, just as you do, only ours are very evolved. We know who we are. We know what we came here to do. Our vision is clear as glass and not cloudy, as yours is. We came to help you peel away the layers of dross that have surrounded your bodies and minds and feelings, so that you can see clearly through the illusion you reside in so that you can get out of the matrix of mass consciousness that is smothering your life force.

We are noticing that you are coming together now in groups, in family units of cooperation to create and work together. This is the purpose of creation—to find each other and create from unity of purpose and unity of strength, so that your creations are magnified ten-fold by the unified

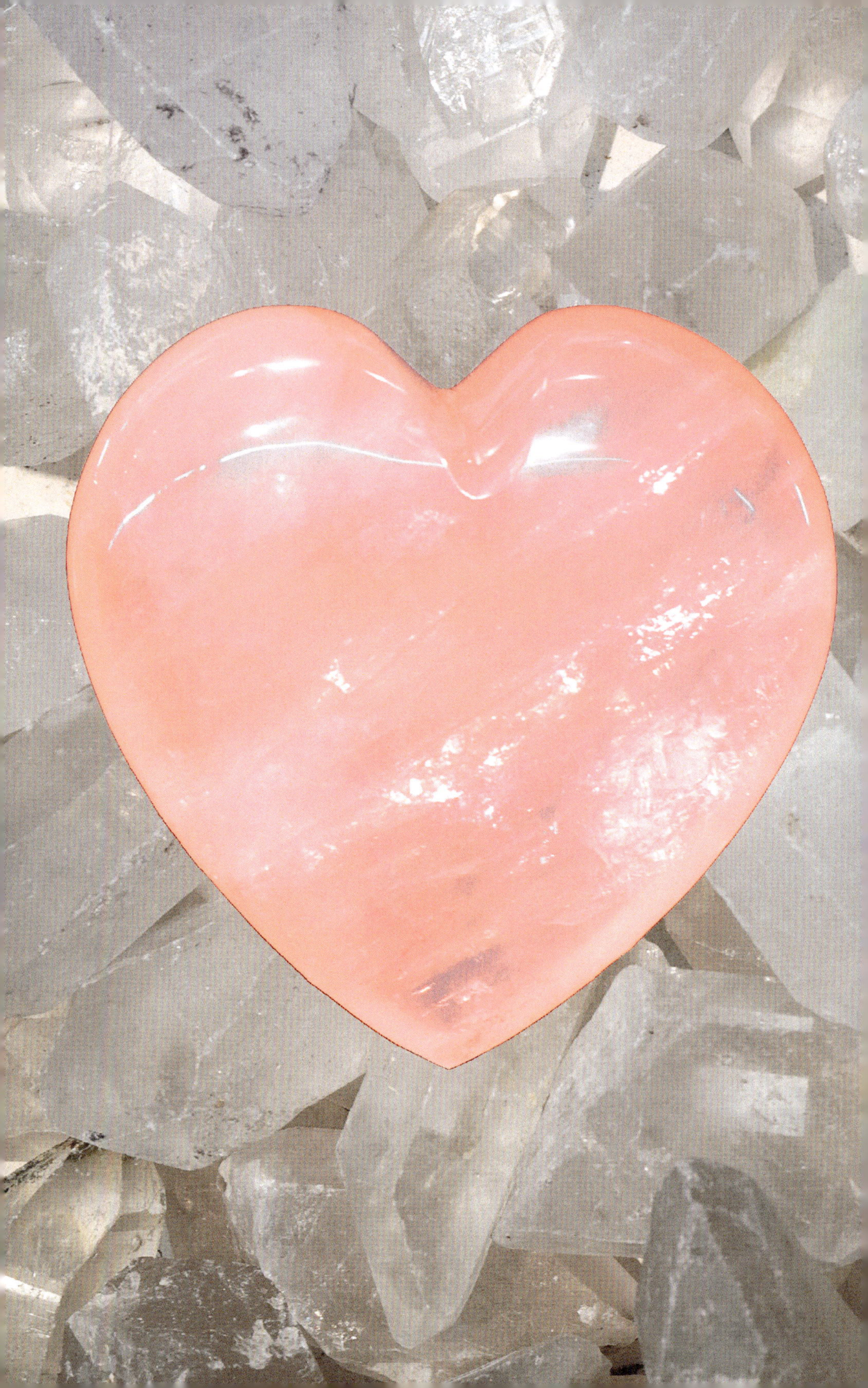

power of your minds and wills. We will help you.

Just hold us in your hands, and ask us to work along with you to magnify and create your intentions so that they manifest in a perfectly formed state, just as you intended and dreamed.

We Crystals are magnificent indeed. We come in all sizes and shapes and hues and colors and frequency ranges. We come from a Crystal System of Worlds, very different from your world. Our world is all Light and all Love, and our Crystal planet's light radiates brilliantly out to the Omniverse, lighting the way for others in need of assistance. Oh, what a glorious sight to behold as you scan our Crystal light rays weaving in and out and around our Omniverse, guiding all who traverse our path to find the light and understanding they are seeking. It is an embrace of love that we shower on all who come our way. Our way is the way of the Creator, who wants his children to be filled with only the love and light that is the creative substance of life.

As you rise in consciousness, you will all find your way to us, as we are beckoning you forth from your cocoon of insulation to open up to the world around you, to the love around you, and to the support that all kingdoms are offering you. Just accept. Once you merge with all of us, you will find the peace you have all been looking for, for it resides in Unity Consciousness. Once you are in Unity Consciousness with all Kingdoms, you are Home. You are then anchored fully in your heart space, where you can travel throughout the Omniverse in your thoughts. It is magical—and you are almost there.

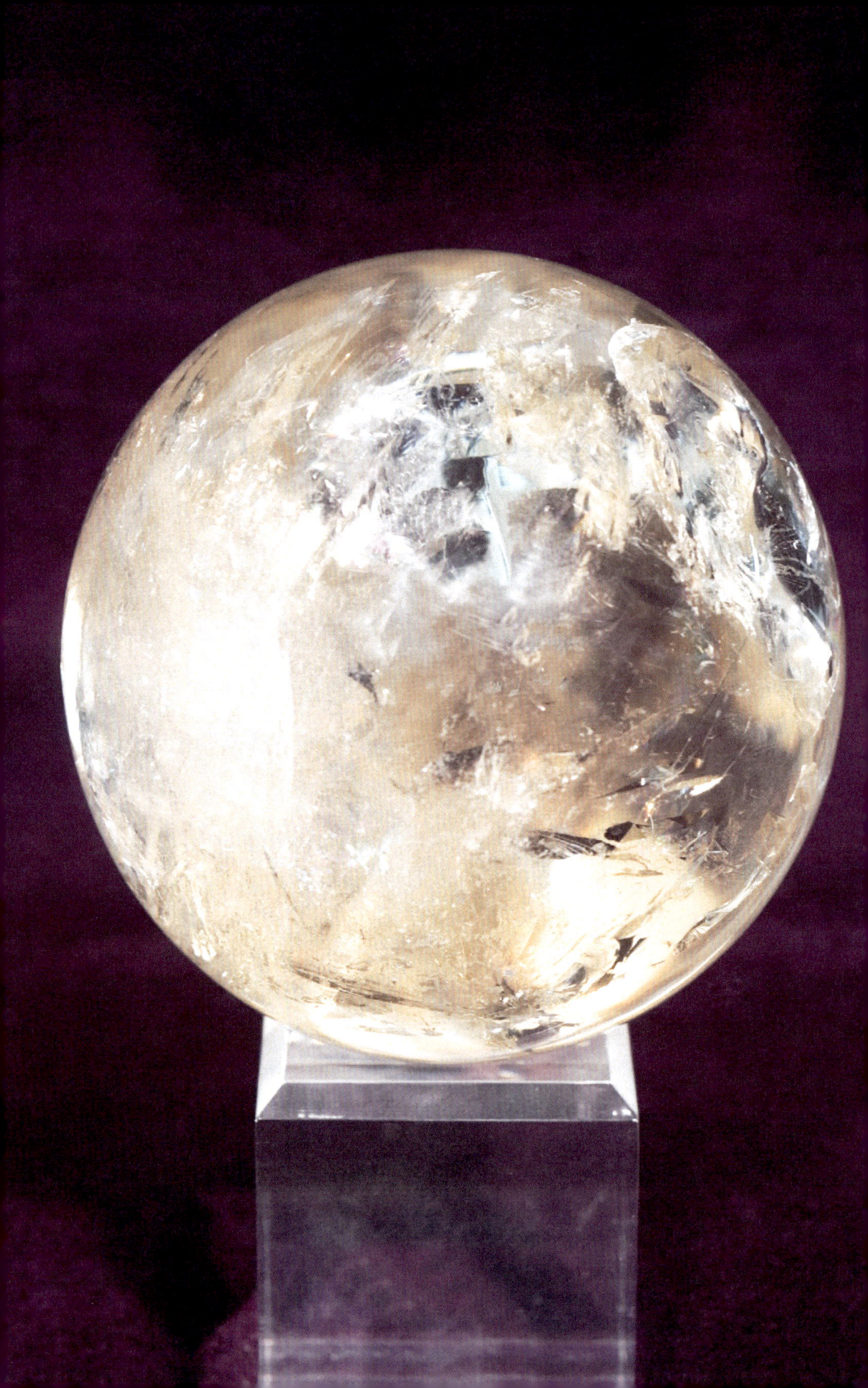

We invite you into our homes. Just hold us and commune with us, as you enter our homes of bliss where we transfer our light quotient directly into your cells on beams of light, to enliven and raise your vibration to match ours.

This is the purpose of Creation—to unite our hearts to reflect the great heart of the Creator within us. It is pure joy, pure ecstasy. Shine with us. We are calling you now.

We wrap you in our rays of Light, and touch your skin and kiss your hands as you hold us close.

We love you,
The Crystals

We Give You a Vibrational Lift

We are the People from the Crystal World, here to speak to you of Love, the love we have for humanity and the love we have for all other life forms. Even though we are encased in hard stone and live in the darkest of realms, we are pure light, and it is soft and dreamy as it flows out from us to all of you. We dream dreams too, and our dreams are about the reuniting of all life forms on and under the surface.

We are ready to have a direct encounter with you, or as you say on the surface, "a first contact" encounter. You think we are inanimate matter, and yet we vibrate at the highest level of vibration, much higher than most humans have attained. When you wear us around your neck or hold us in your hand, your electrons then start to raise their vibration to match ours,

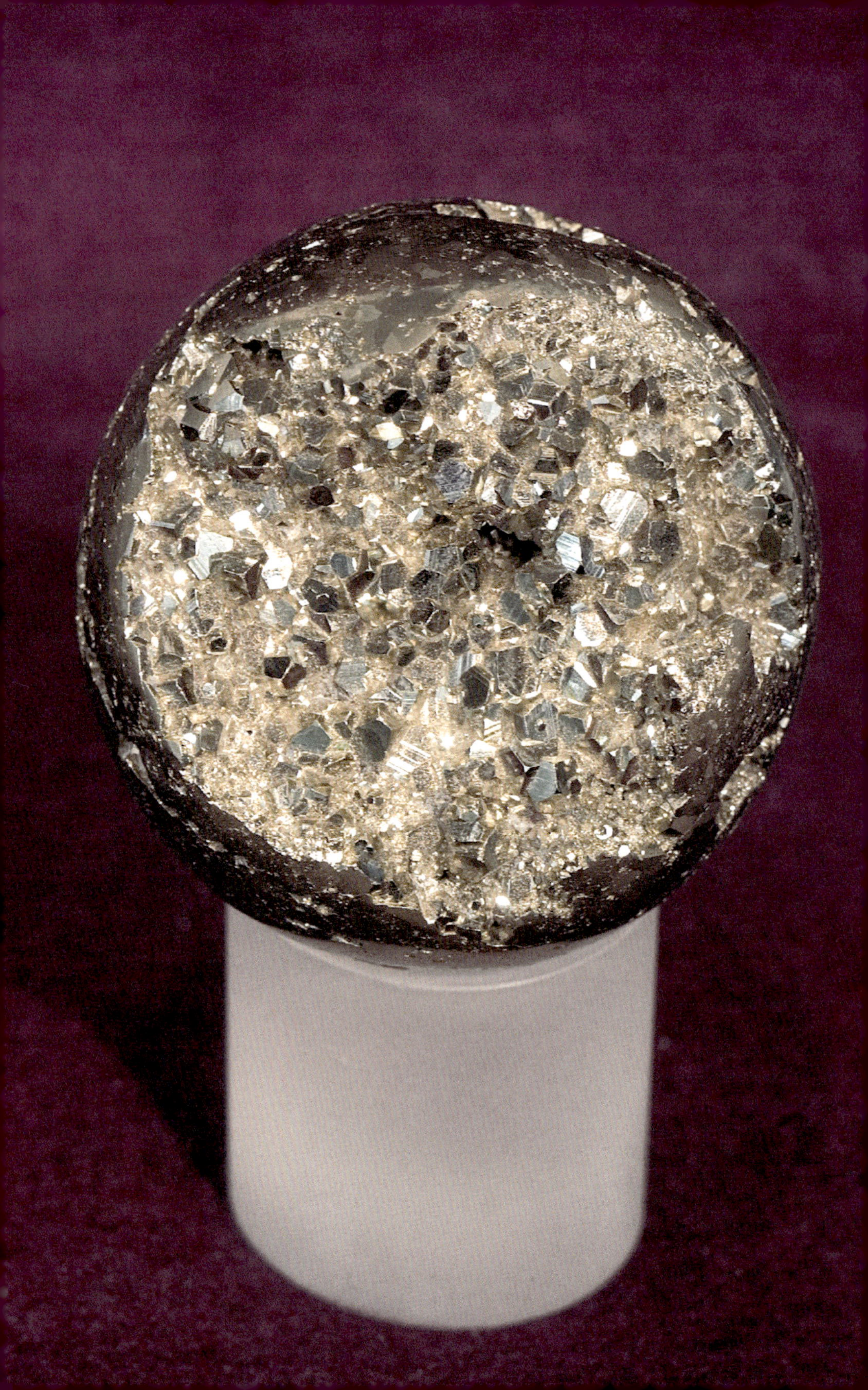

and you are given a vibrational lift moving you closer to the 5th dimension vibration of unconditional love.

So hold us close, and love us, as we love you. All is shifting now on your world. All is in change, even now as we speak, although the results are not yet obvious to your eyes. But we have 5th dimensional eyes, and we can see into the future, and we see the immense and drastic changes about to take place. It is all about consciousness.

We are here to boost your consciousness level and help you see and hear the world around you. For up until now you have been deaf to our calls, and to the calls from the Trees and the myriad of other life forms calling to you to "wake up" and be part of the intricate matrix of life on Earth. Up until now you have always been separate, seeing yourselves as the overlords of the world, when in actuality your purpose was to work with all other life forms, not to destroy them in your quest for money.

It is sad that you had lost your way, but the tide is turning, and you will soon see the unseen, and know the unknowing, and then you will find yourselves and realize how much more there is to life than just making money. As your saying from the past went, "Make love, not money," you will see how "love" will create all the wealth you have been seeking. What a twist in thinking, isn't it? You can lay greed and struggle to rest, and accomplish all you desire through your love. It is much easier, and feels so much better.

In the Crystal World, we accomplish all we desire through our great outpouring of love. We don't have to go anywhere

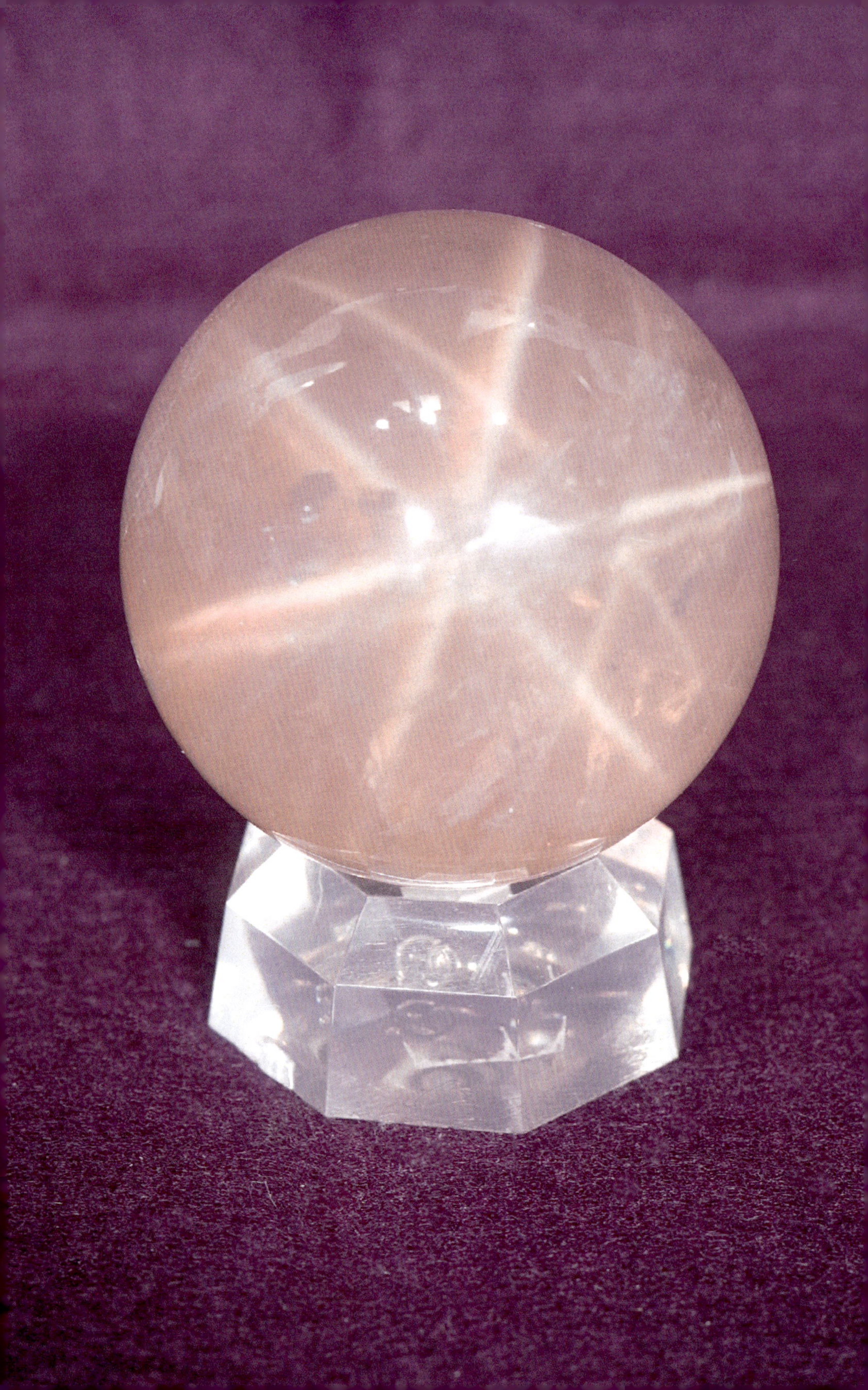

or do anything, we just emit our love rays and everything is accomplished. **It is these rays that you will discover and learn to project from your brow that will bring you your desires.** But your hearts and intentions must be pure in order to create from your light rays. This is what we are here to teach you, if you follow our ways and join with us in consciousness. As you follow our ways, your rays will ignite until you are as clear and bright as we are. Then together we will light up the Earth, and a great re-union will occur. It is this reunion of all life forms on Earth that will catapult you all into the 5th dimension.

Divine alignment is the key. So align with your divinity, and as you do, you will find us all aligned with you. We bid you good day.

We Are Film Makers

Greetings, our dearest friend on Earth. We are the Crystal People, all decked out in our finest orbs of Light to greet you.

Our lives are blissful and peaceful, and we radiate quantum amounts of light energy into the Earth and onto the surface for all life forms to use. We give freely of all our light, and in return all we need comes back to us in greater amounts than we give out. This is the way of all life. The more you give, the more you receive. It is a Universal Law. It is what Jesus spoke about.

You can feel our energy surrounding you. It is our love

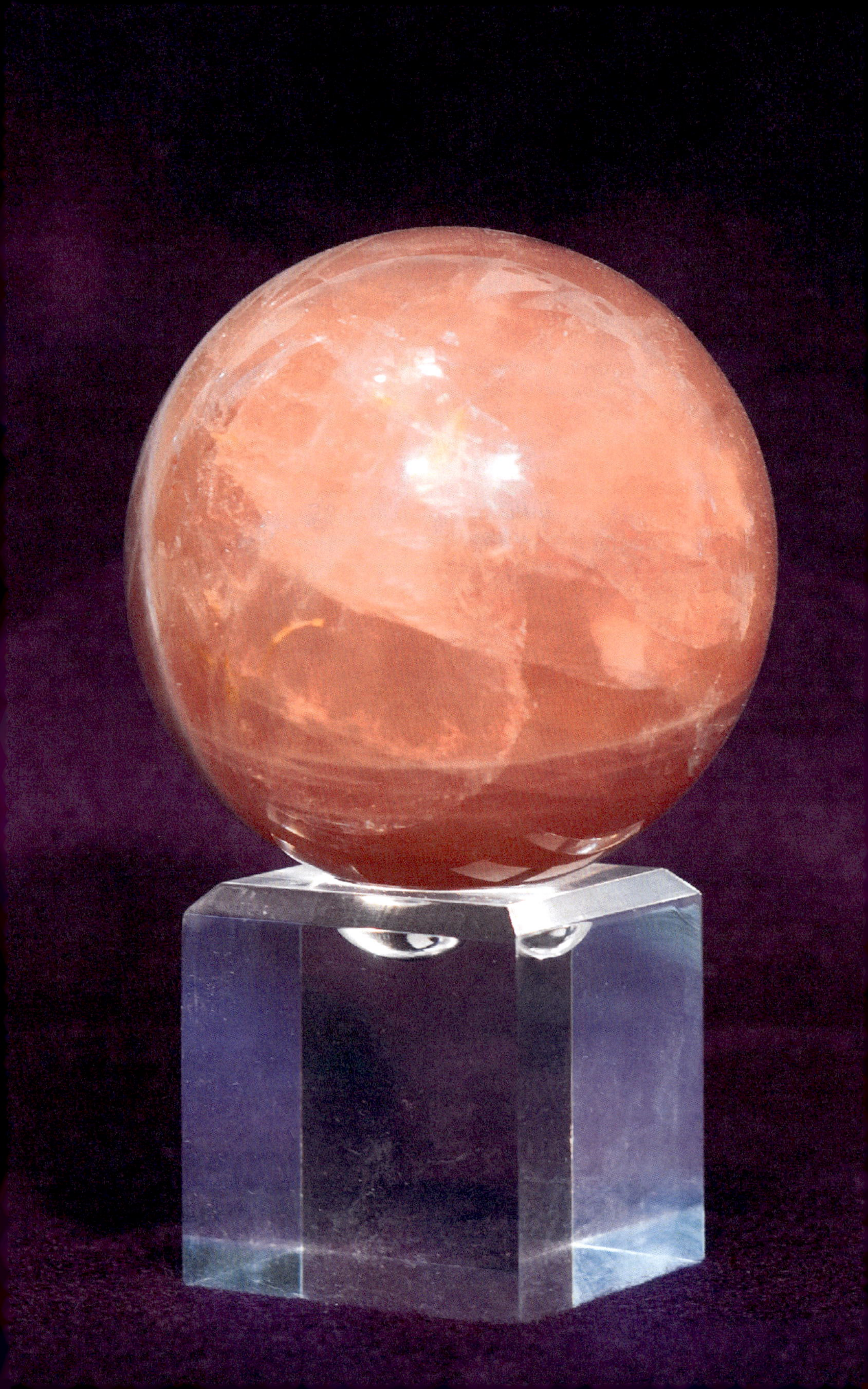

swirling around you. We can feel yours too. It is a deep connection between us.

Today we will talk about love. Love of self and love of the Creator. It is love that moves the stars, and love that sustains Creation. The Creator is all love. Love is all there is. The more you love, the more you create. The more you create, the more you contribute to creation. Creation is expansion. Everything is in a state of expansion, even the Crystal Kingdom. We are ever expanding in our knowledge and wisdom, even though we do this in the depths of the Earth.

Deep in the Earth is a tranquility beyond anything you can imagine. It is serene. It is peace. It is expansive. It allows us to fly in our thoughts instantaneously. The air waves are clear, with no impediments. Yes, there is air deep in the Earth, although different from what you breathe.

Our homes are tucked deep underground, and our families are all joined together. We don't move away from each other like you do. We remain where we are born. This way, we can create cohesive communities that are "tight knit" and strong and supportive—knowing that we each will always be there for one another. Most lifeforms in the Inner Earth follow this community living arrangement. There's no need for physical moving, as we can move our consciousness at "will." This is the true way of traveling.

Great amounts of Light are now seeping into the Earth…or should we say "plummeting down" from the Great Central Sun to awaken humans. There is a great outpouring of love and light from the Heaven Realms, and more Beings involved in Earth's

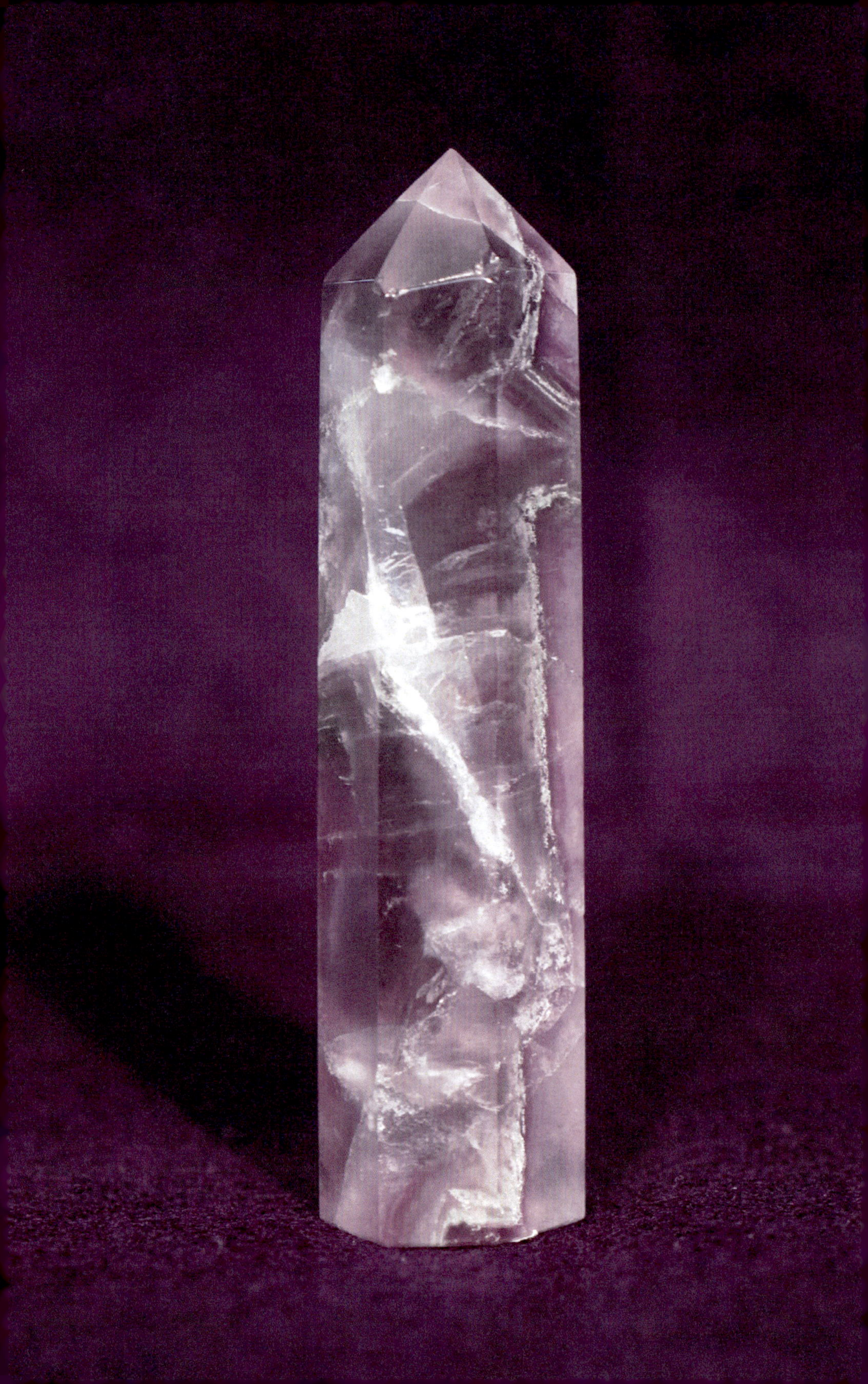

ascension than you can imagine. Beings are here from all over the Galaxy and beyond. They are all watching, all waiting, and all beaming their love to you. It is quite a show.

We, in the Crystal World, are part of this great show. We are the photographers, of sort, capturing pictures in our crystalline matrix and saving them to show you when you learn to play us back on Crystal Projectors — and we don't "run out of film." What a show you will see — and you are the actors and actresses playing the roles. So dress up in your finest and best, and play your roles in the purest integrity…for you are indeed captured on "camera"…for all of posterity to see.

This makes things different, doesn't it? It changes the way you go about your life…when you know you are being filmed and all of creation has access to the movie. This heightens your awareness of yourself, and you then watch yourself act out your life with others — in the very moment it is happening. You cannot erase a line, or delete a scene in your daily movement and encounters with others, for we capture it as it happens…and there's no editing.

So knowing this, we hope it will serve as a constant reminder that every word and action you take affects others. Just the way you look at others affects them.

We don't have to be in your hands to record your words… they flow out to us, where we pick up the sound and feeling. You are being filmed on so many levels. If humans only knew this, they would certainly stop to think before they spoke, and would weigh their words and nuances of speech. There is so much involved in your encounters with others…beyond what

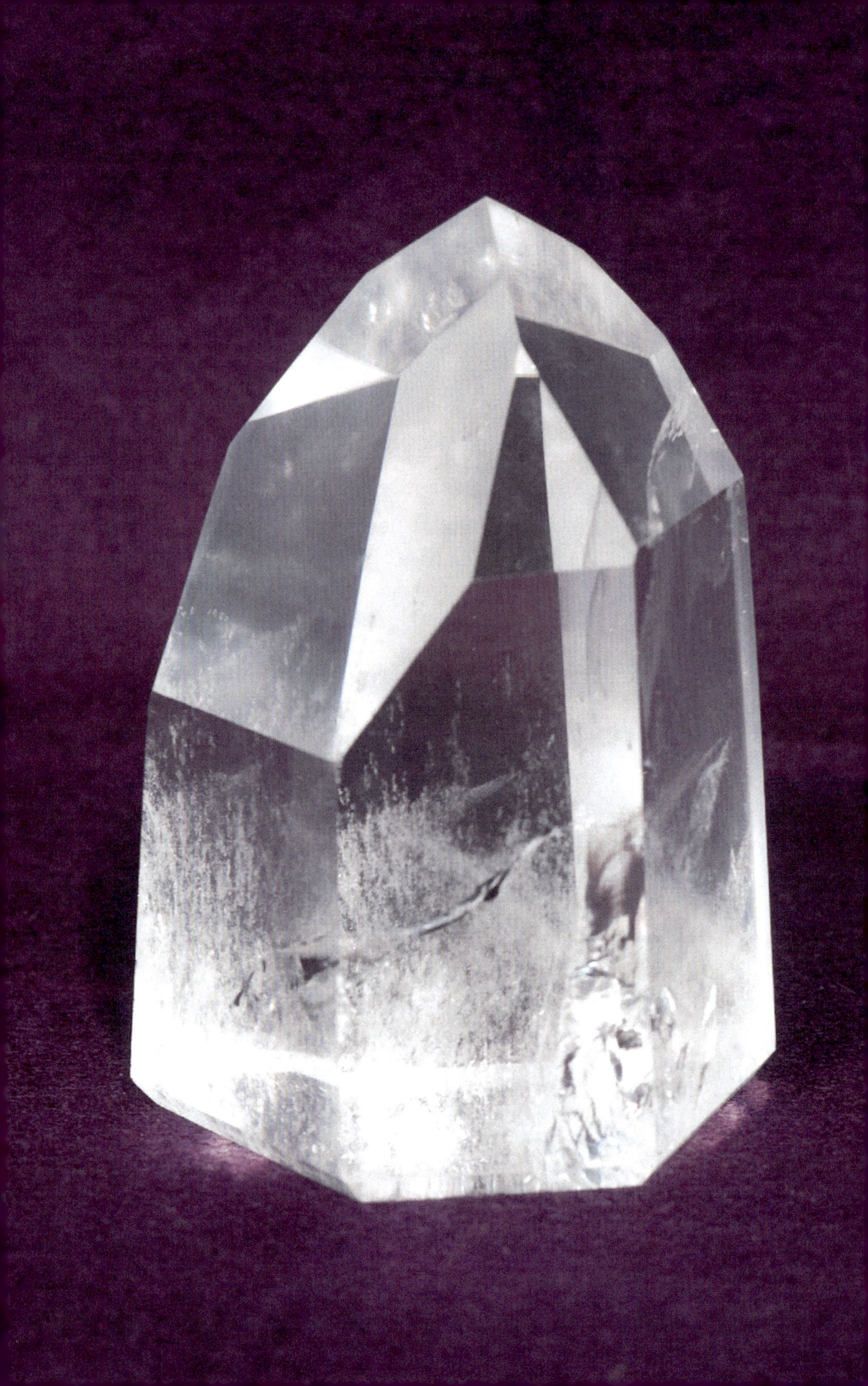

you can see. But we can see it all…buried as we are deep in the Earth. So location doesn't matter. It is our spirits that have no bounds. We are truly "free spirits"…all of us.

We close now, and thank you for coming to your computer to commune with us. We await our next encounter with anticipation.

We love you,
The Crystal People

Bliss Is the Great Indicator of Light

We came to Earth millions of years ago from a far distant star system to help "lighten" the planet and help humans rise in consciousness. We thought our beauty and shape would entice humans to hold us and wear us, and thus enhance their auras with our light frequency that spills out from our encasement…for our encasement is "porous", you might say, even though it feels hard to your touch. Just being in our vicinity enables you to absorb our light waves to increase yours…and increase you must…for you've fallen behind the other kingdoms in consciousness, and it is late in the game and time to restore and rebuild your light quotient so you can "fly" with us into higher realms and commune with us as easily as you can talk to each other.

Life is moving up the consciousness grid rapidly now, and all are preparing for the great rebirth into Light…the Light of divine creation where we all merge as One. We beckon you

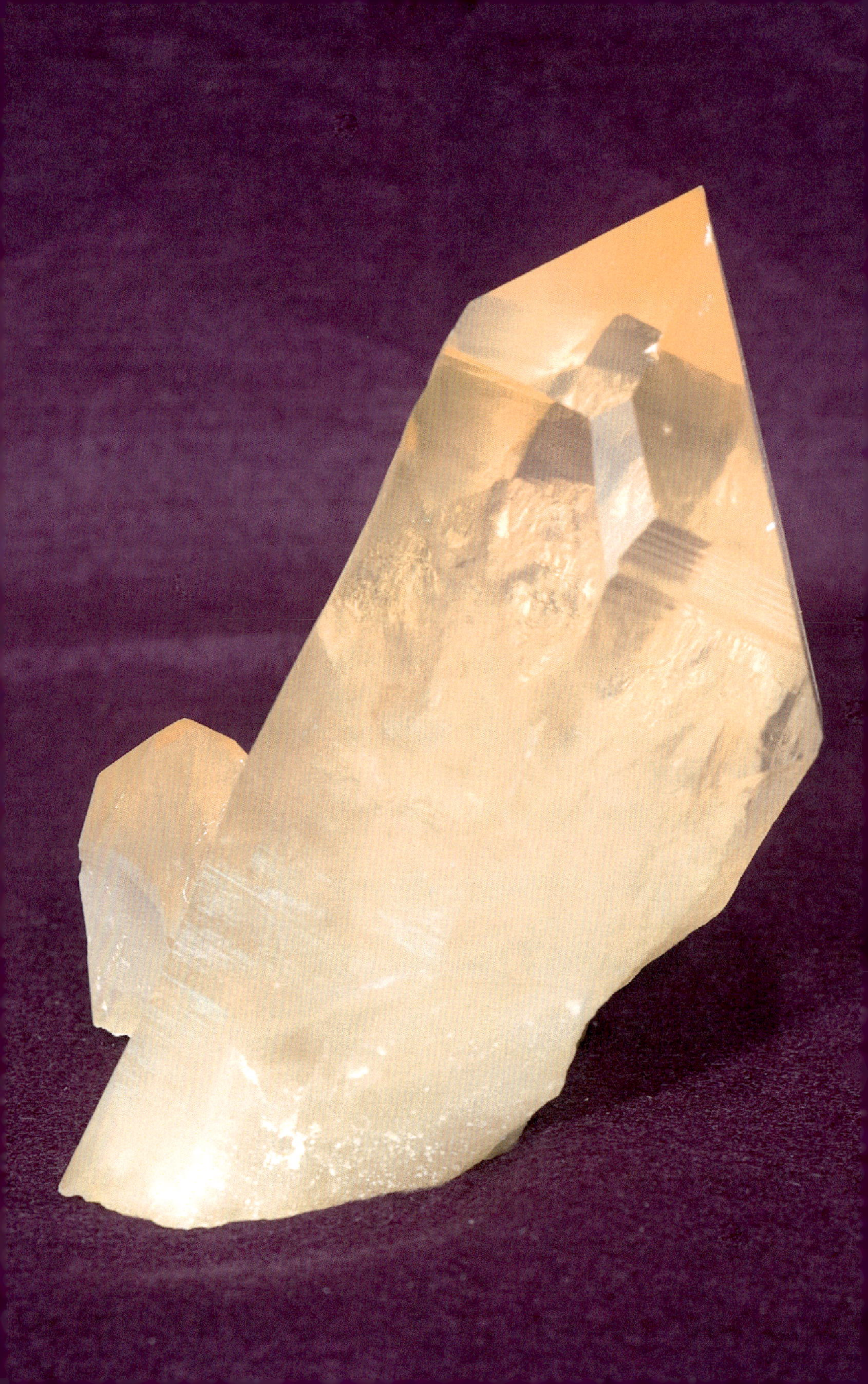

to join us. You have been the missing component, and we've missed you. We entreat you to use our Light to help you boost your light quotient by keeping us in your homes and wearing us around your neck and carrying us in your pockets. We, too, are your brothers and sisters, although we don't have gender as you do. We are all multi-gendered and multi-faceted and multi-tasked "people"…waiting to merge our consciousness with you into One.

There is no time to lose, even though there is "no time." Your time, as you know it, is rapidly collapsing. You are now in 2012, when all kingdoms will move up in bliss as One. For the more Light you carry, the more "bliss" you feel…bliss is the great indicator of Light, and indicates or registers how much Light you are carrying. Did you know that?

Ah, our dear children of Earth, how we have missed your communion, and how we yearn to commune with you to establish One Kingdom on Earth, the Kingdom of God in all its many facets and many forms, all united into One heart, One song, One brilliant rainbow of Light reverberating out into our Universe, letting all other life forms know that we have unified our many selves into the wholeness of Creation by reuniting with the Creator.

We sing our praises to you, our soul sisters and brothers, for our souls match yours, only in a different form. Come and find us, for we wait for you to pick us up and hold us tenderly in your hands as we warm your hearts and cherish your touch.

We love you,
The Crystal People

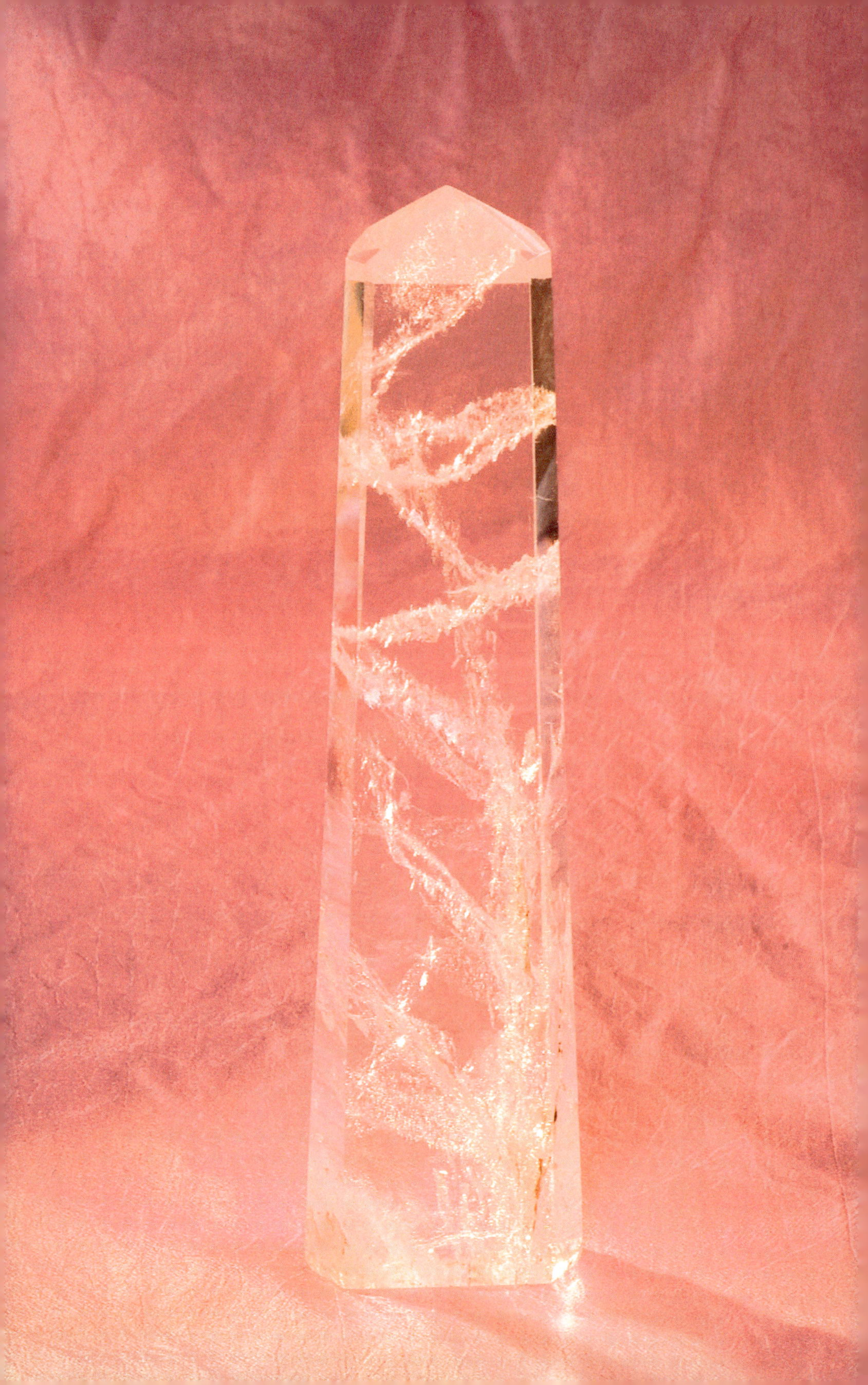

Changeover to an Immortal Body of Crystalline Light

Greetings from the World of Crystals.

We are the Crystal People, and we are gathered around you. We love you. Do you know that you are also composed of crystalline light substance? Yes, you are. Only your bodies have densified the Light that you are, into physical substance, physical matter, to encase your embodiment in this 3rd dimensional realm, for you couldn't maneuver and operate in this realm if you were pure light substance. You needed a densified body to fully experience all the delights on Earth. Earth is composed of matter, the same matter as your body composition. So you are One.

However, we in the Crystal World have held our form of Pure Crystalline Light Substance, and it is this Light that we shower upon you, as you go about your business on the surface—hurrying and scurrying through "time." We don't hurry and scurry—we just stand still, and yet are able to be wherever we want to be and when we want to be there. It is quite a delightful existence.

So, back to the crystalline light bodies that you are. Before you alighted on this planet, you were all Light. Your bodies had to take on a denser composition in order to maneuver here, and to partake of all the wonders that were created for you to experience. You came to jump into densified matter and to experience it all. However, there was one shortcoming in all

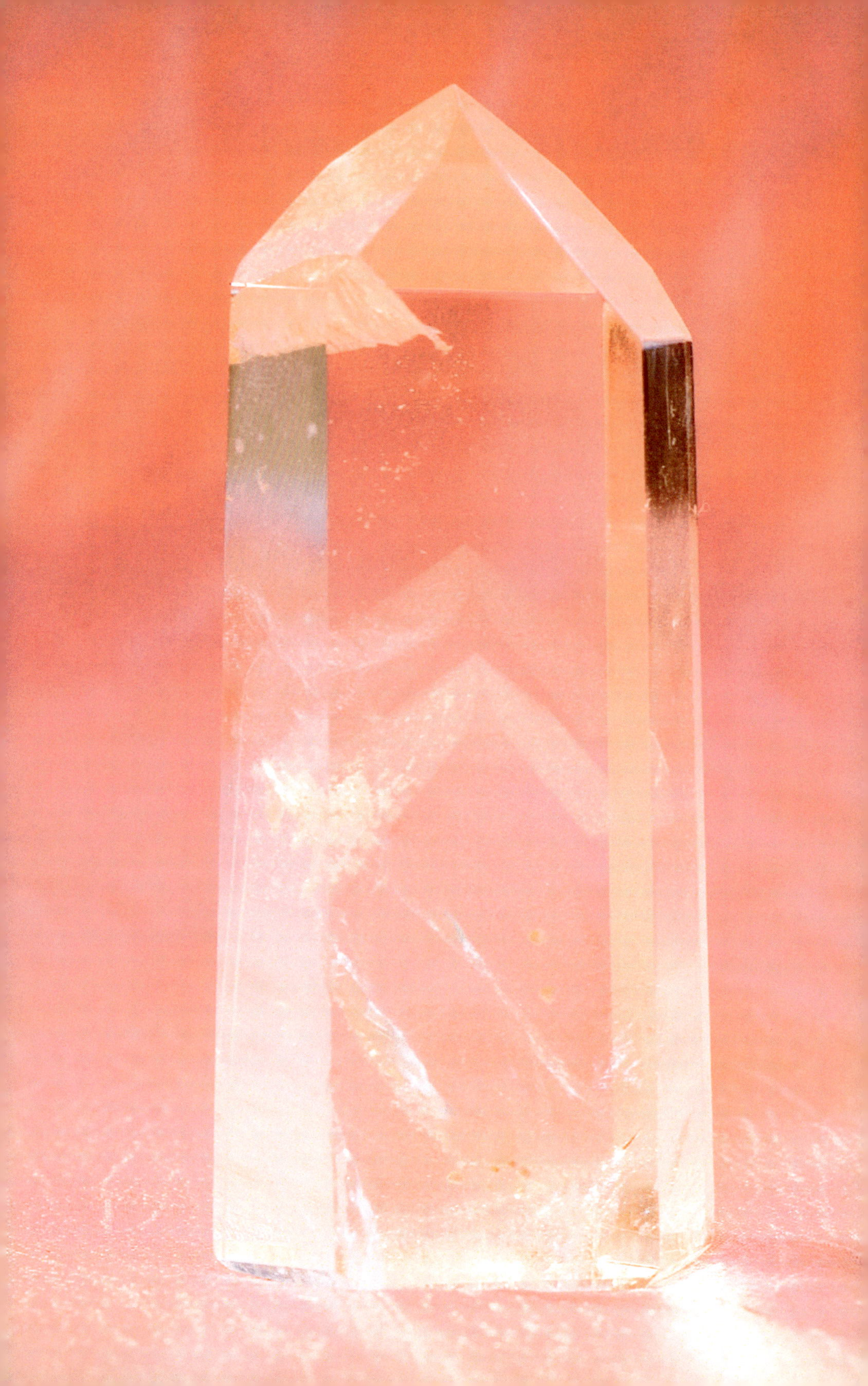

of this—you lost your way. But that is over now, and you are slowly regaining your identity, and your density is now recapturing your Light. Your cells are transmuting into crystalline light particles now, and we in the Crystal world are assisting. This is why it is crucial for you to connect with us on our wavelength, which is in a higher octave. <u>We can help lift you up to meet our electron spin. Our electron spin is spinning on currents of Light and these waves will connect with you and transmute your physical matter into crystalline light particles</u>.

It is pure alchemy, and we are here to assist you in your changeover to an immortal body of Crystalline Light. Oh my, what a ride you are in for. You are beginning to ride the waves of crystalline light, carrying you closer and closer to your divine self. In the Crystal World, we all know we are divine. We commune with the divinity in each of you, as you hold us in your hands or sleep with us on your bodies. We commune with you from great distances and depths, when you think of us—for your thoughts reach through the ethers to us, and we send you back our love and light waves. All life on Earth connects like this. <u>It is "thought" connection—the fastest kind of communication in existence.</u>

<u>All life in our Galaxy is linked through "thought" waves. And you have it built right into you. Cell phones and email will soon be replaced by your own telecommunications network</u>. You will be able to contact anyone, in any location in time and space, on or off your home planetary system. You will be taking the human form to greater heights, never reached in times before. You are in the process of creating

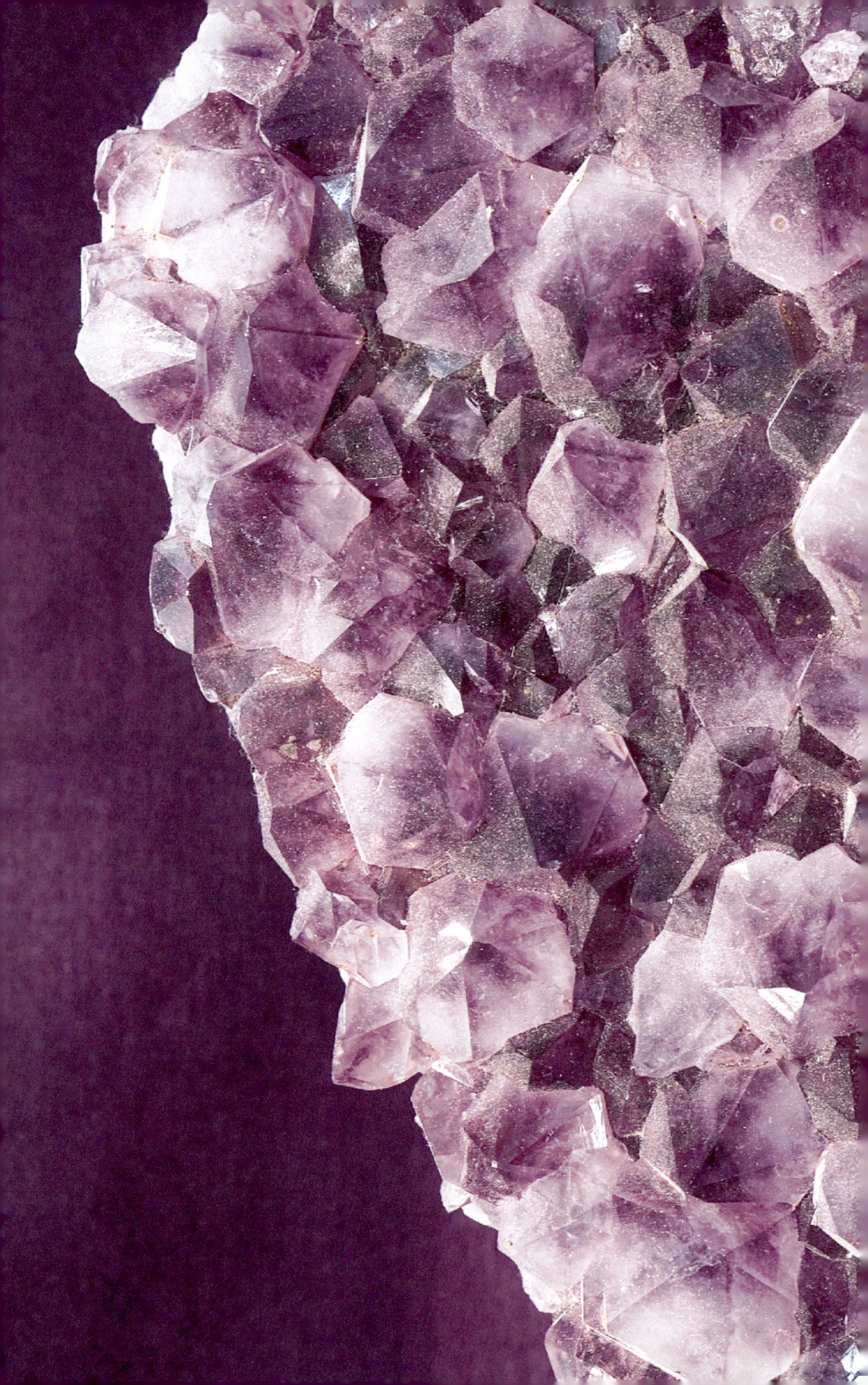

the **"immortal human"** encased in light substance, living on a physical planet and being able to move in and out of density. What a trip you are in for! The beauty of all of this, is that all other life forms ride along with you to experience new delights of existence.

We leave you for now, and request your connection to our hearts. Yes, we too have hearts, and when you think of us, our hearts light up into flames. So fan our hearts with your thoughts and we will send our heart flames to you. Catch the light.

We are the Crystal People, and we bid you good day.

We Hold the Crystalline Matrix of your Universe

Greetings, our dear sister on Earth. We are the Crystal People here again with you as you sit at your computer taking our dictation. We are very close to you, as close as your life vein pulsing blood into your system. We breathe with you, we pulse our heartbeat with you, and we sing our Song of the Ages to you. Our song is Love…and its melody permeates your cells as we merge into you now. Our merging is complete—and we operate as One.

Crystals are unique in character, as their Light is so bright that your eyes could be blinded could you look into our depths. Our depths hold the crystalline matrix of your universe, unraveled in its complexity and structure. It is your guide to everywhere, could you but read its map. Your body is also a map,

Bubbles Inside a Crystal

with life codes embedded in your DNA strands. Your body has a blueprint that can replicate itself into perfection, were it not tampered with, and were it not for the stress and fear you have all brought into it. Stress and fear only deteriorate its precise mechanisms, and keep you from attaining your immortality.

We Crystals do not hold stress or fear. Actually, it is entirely unknown to us, for our Light Quotient is so high that we only experience Divine Love. When you only focus on your Divinity, there can be no room for any other feeling or thought to exist, and that is when your heart opens to your I AM Presence and you feel the joy of union and completeness.

So it is all in your thoughts and focus that you can move yourself into your Divinity, for your thoughts will carry you to wherever you direct them. So direct them to your God Self, and feel them uniting you to All That Is: your Inner Light in your heart that is waiting for you to acknowledge its Presence. Stay in your heart space, and feel only the JOY of life, only the LOVE of the Creator, only the PURITY of your I AM Presence, and beckon them in. Stay with the Music of the Spheres, and it will re-calibrate your cells to the Music of Home. Home is in the heart—and you already know this.

You find your way back Home through your Heart. It is the quickest route to the Ascension, and we await you there. We are already stationed in your heart, and we wait for your call to accompany you on your trip back to Unity Consciousness. We will carry you along with us, if you only acknowledge our existence as fellow travelers on the road through Eternity.

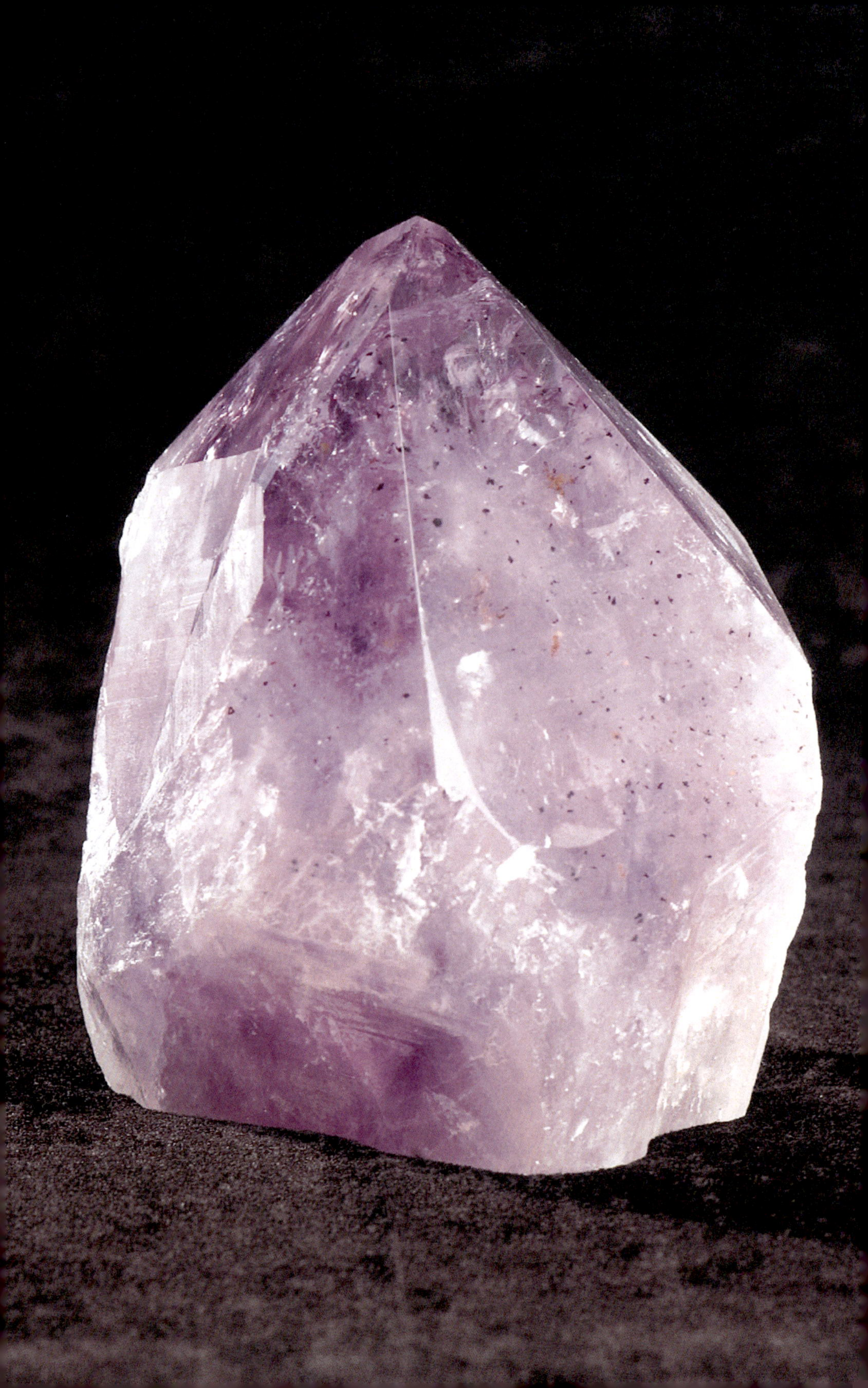

As you hold and caress us in your hands, <u>we re-calibrate your life pulse</u>, so that you can beat with the rest of life on Earth and merge with us in the One Beat of Creation, all vibrating at the same frequency. This is the quickest way for all of us to ascend, for our ascension is not complete without your accompaniment. **ALL OF CREATION TRAVELS TOGETHER.** We not only need one another, but we are one another. Once you wake up to our existence and to the fact that we have been trying to contact you for millennia, we can begin our merging of consciousness and move up to a higher octave of existence. We wait for your call.

Once you merge with us, you will quickly discover how to use and harness our Light and Energy to convert your antiquated fossil fuel system into Free Energy for everyone on the planet. This will be a big step for mankind, for the patriarchal system of control and corruption will be out of business and the Divine Feminine will flow through your veins, bringing you all that is your birthright, and it is all free.

Earth has provided all you could ever conceive of, and gives it freely. You just have to open to its existence, and allow and accept it to flow to you, unimpeded by doubt or fear. This is why it is so important to rein in your thoughts and stay only in the Love Vibration, for Love will bring you to the treasures that Earth has been storing for you. There is a treasure chest just waiting for you to open, and you open it with your Heart—just let it all burst free.

Hold us, talk to us, and we will be your guides taking you into the Light where we already reside. Join us.

We are the Crystal People.

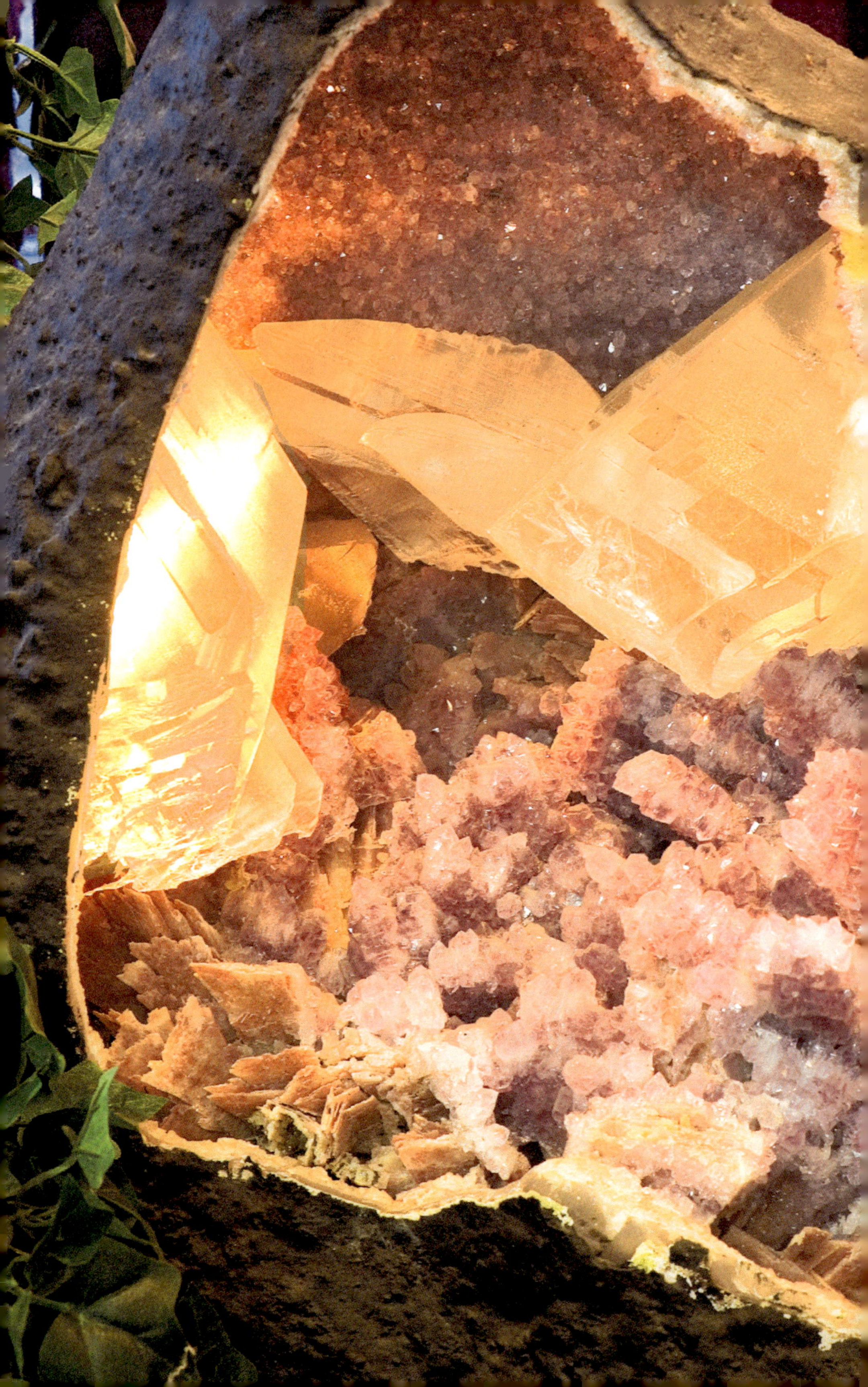

We Once Powered the Whole Planet

Greetings, our dearest soul daughter on Earth. We are the Crystal Kingdom, yearning to continue our dialogue with you. Know that we do remember the times when we were above ground, and our structures towered above the surface like gigantic skyscrapers overhead. We powered the whole planet then, in every aspect of its energy requirements. We did it all, with very little effort on our part, and with no residue or side effects to the environment. Our energy transmissions are the cleanest, purest, and most pristine way to harness energy for your consumption.

We captured all the historic records from these times past, and we still hold them in our energy matrix although we are now in seclusion underground until it is safe for us to rise again in all our majesty and glory.

Safety is still an issue for us, for we don't want to be intruded upon or damaged or pillaged. The Earth needs us just where we are—for we continue to do our work underground and act as great electronic relay stations that transmit information on many levels to the Galactic Command and Mother Earth. We work "undercover" or "underground", in the privacy of our own domain. We, too, work for the Ashtar Command and Spiritual Hierarchy of the planet, and our work uncovers the deepest information that we make available to the Forces of Light who tap into us.

Earth has provided all to her residents, even free energy.

There is free energy for everything you could ever need or dream of. You just have to tap into us, the Crystal Kingdom, and we will show you how to harness our light and change it into energy. It is so easy to do, once your desire is there, and there is no more interference from the sinister forces who would only corrupt our gift to you and turn it against you, and all life, in their endeavor to enslave all of humanity in their quest for conquest.

Our love goes out to you on waves of crystalline light beams, and embraces you.

Poetry Is Our Specialty

We are the Crystals
We carry pure light
It's just our depth
That is out of your sight

We are buried so deeply, down in the ground
So that we can, not be found

For our power is awesome
And our Light is so bright
That if you found us now
It would cause such a fright

We once powered your planet
And gave freely our Light
But humans misused us
So we now live far from your sight

Our depth is our security
It is dark and deep
And you will find us when
You awaken from your sleep

The time is coming
When you will discover our gifts
For we will give you all
A vibrational lift

That will boost your planet
And help Her shift
So you will no longer be
Cast adrift

But ride the currents
Of our light
Until you have again, regained, your inner sight
And move back into the realms of Creator's light

The time to find us
Will be coming soon
Our gigantic size and awesome power
Will be a boon

For we can supply you with all the energy
That you now consume
And light your planet
As the Sun lights the Moon

Just hold us and caress us
And keep us near
For we can lighten your hearts
And fill you with cheer

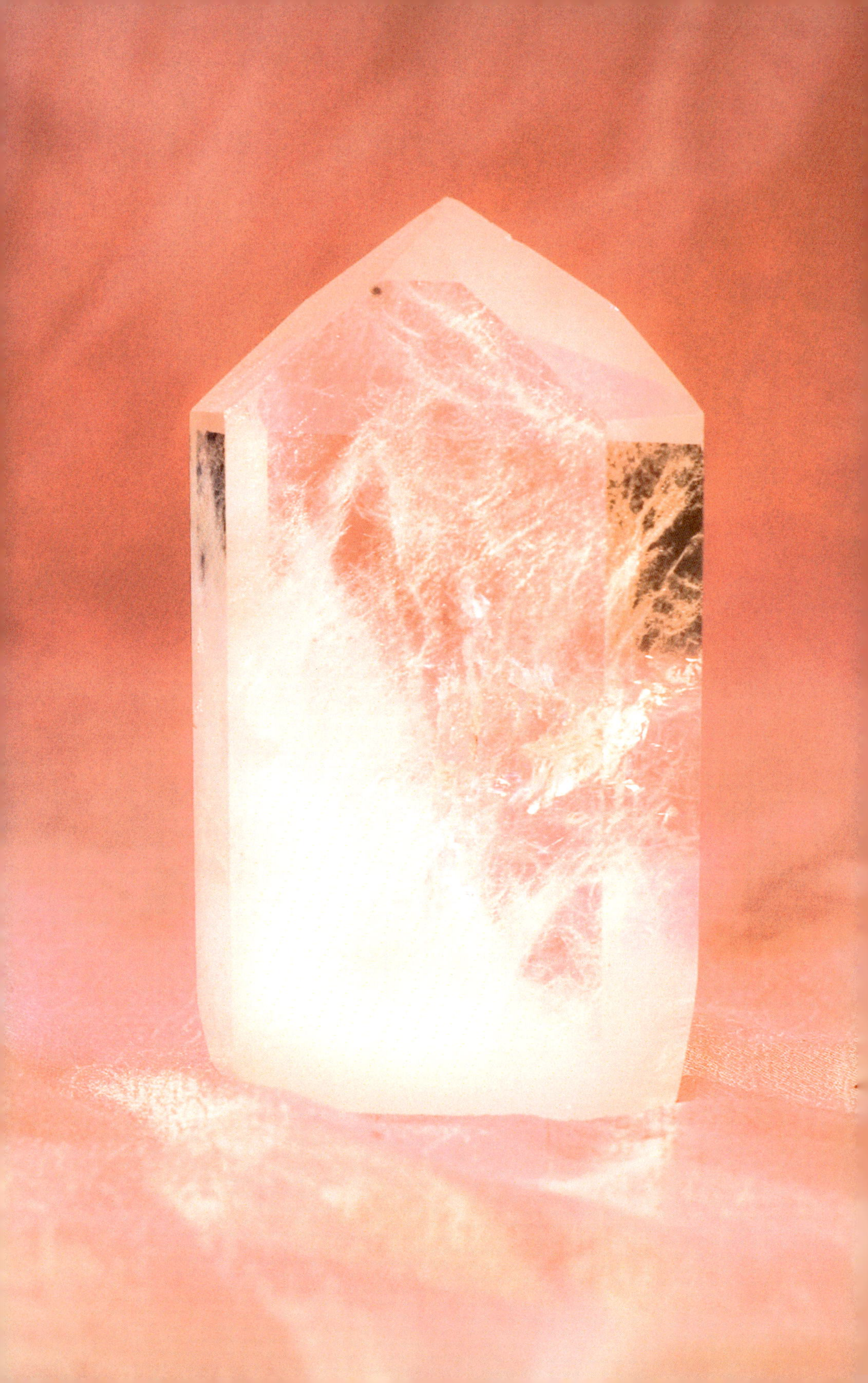

For our composition is purity
And our Light is so clear
That by holding us close to you
We can erase all your fear

We are clearer than glass
And our brilliance and glow
Will always last

We are Power and Light
And can supply all your needs
You just have to call to us
We are ready to please

We don't burn out
We glow like the Sun
And when you discover our uses
You will have such fun

We can light your way
And guide your thoughts
So that you can, become, what you ought
To be—which is free

From energy bills
And planetary ills
And reap the benefits
Of power unlimited

By connecting with us
And discovering our gifts
You can, make, this mighty shift
Into the 7th Great Golden Crystal Age
That, will, be the rage!

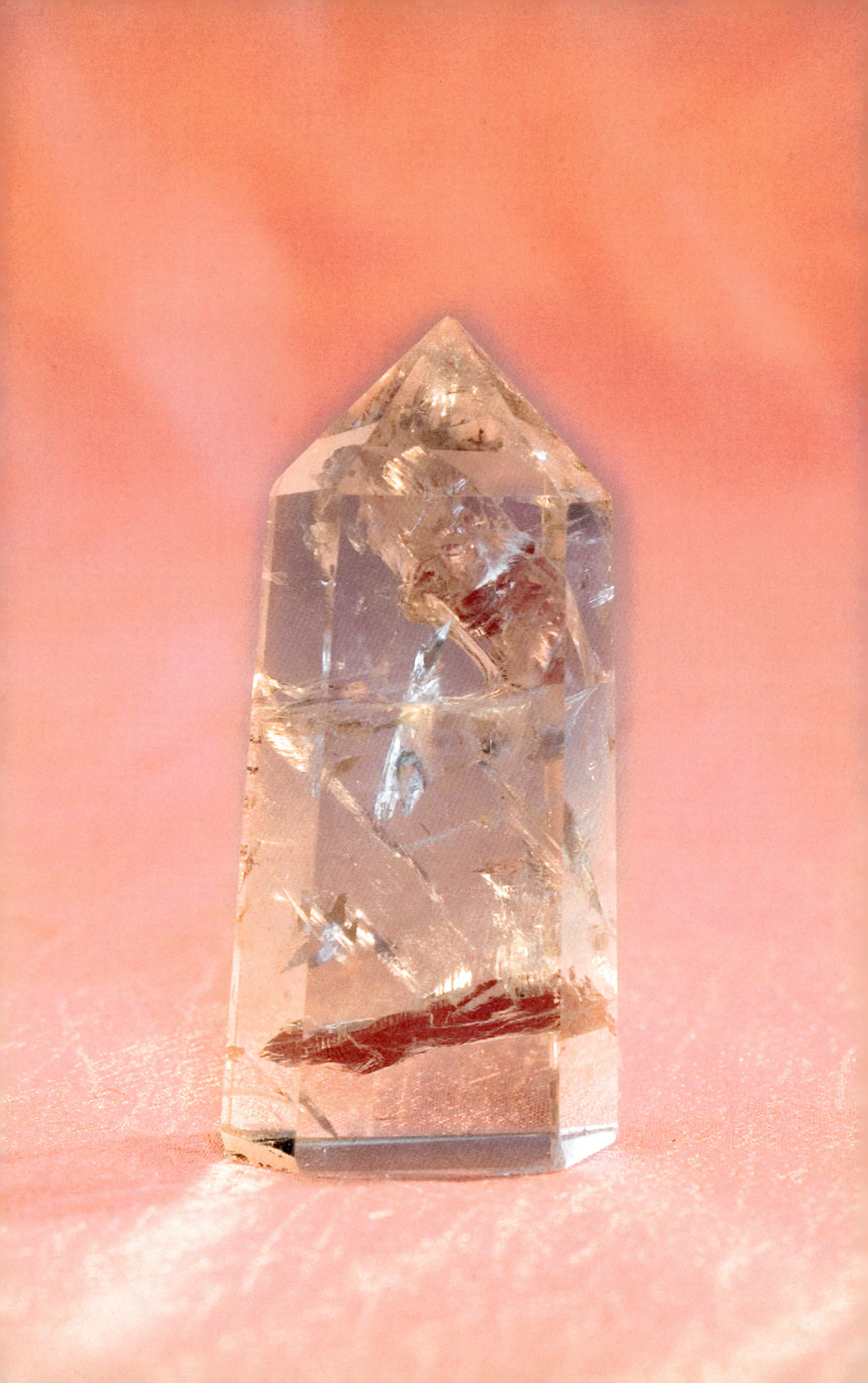

Where all you desire and all your needs
Will be supplied to you with grace and ease

Your Earth is waiting
For you to achieve
Your light and brilliance
So She can leave

And move with our Universe
To heights yet unknown
And move you all up into a higher
Vibrational zone

Called "Home"

Our crystalline light
Will help you regain your sight
So carry us with you, and put us in your homes
And we promise you that, you will never feel alone

For we are your new companions
Your partners on Earth
And this is the moment
Of your rebirth

Into the Creator Beings
You were meant to be
And we are here to help
Set you free

We hold the matrix of the Universe
In our crystalline web
A crystal ball to hold
As you rest in your bed

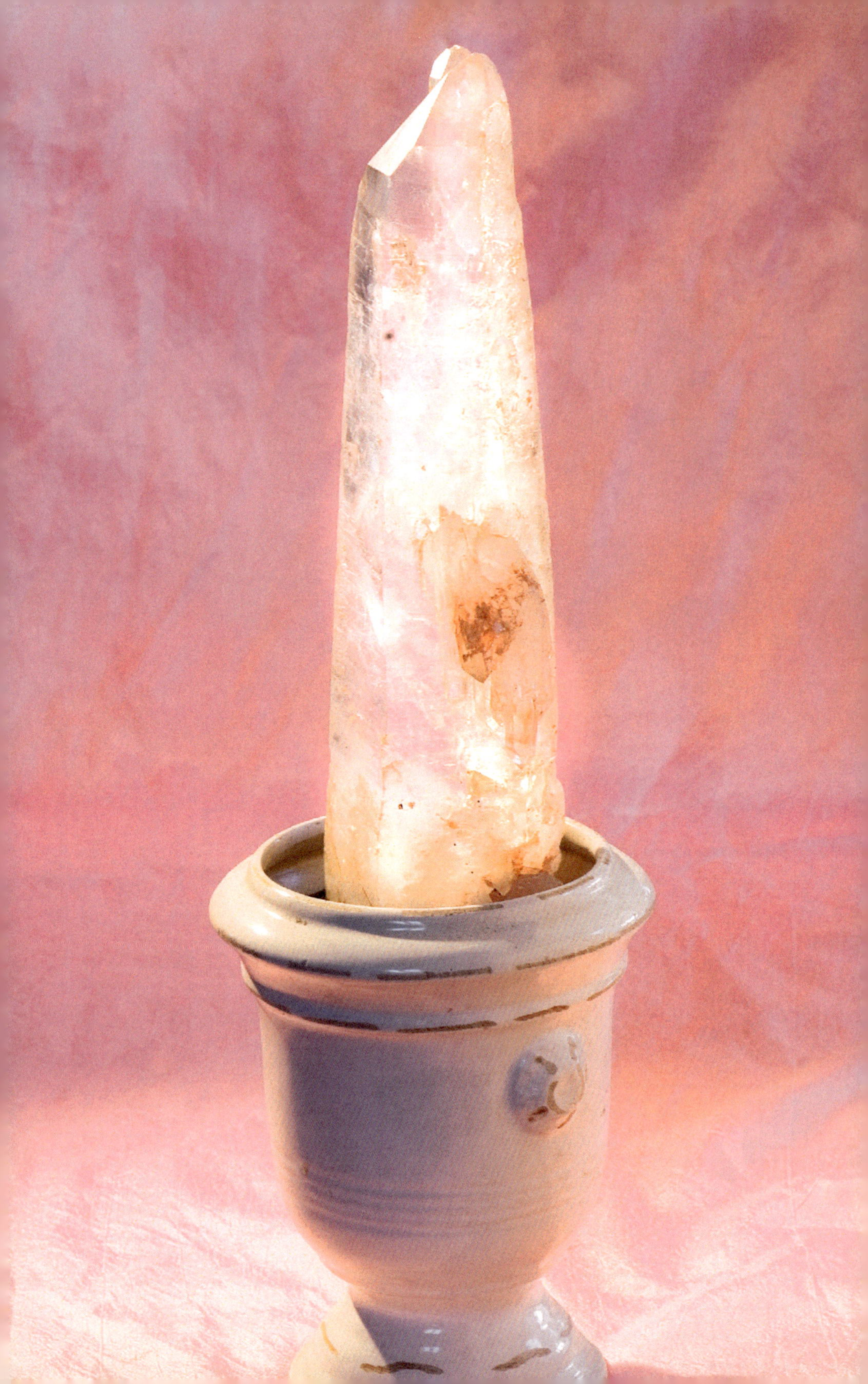

We Crystals are here
To guide your way
So that you will not falter or be swayed
Just touch us and sleep with us
And talk to us each day

We are your Guides
Living with you on Earth
And it is time to connect with us and not travel alone
Just call to us on, the telepathic phone

We can hear your thoughts
And send you ours
For we are not very far
Time between us does not exist
If you remember that distance
Is just a myth

The Universe is waiting
Do you hear Her "call?"
For we are all ready
To come to you all
And erase the memory
Of the "Fall"

And carry you with us into new heights
Where you discover new clarity and sight
And wonder how you ever fell from such a great height

Well, that is all over
The spell is in the past
And now it's 10,000 years of peace at last

That will not cease
Until all life forms have been released

From bondage and struggle
And every other trouble
That never was, meant to be
And again you'll become totally free

We Crystals will help you, to find your way
Just carry us with you, and don't delay
Put us in your pockets, and water you drink
And we will guide you, as you think

And your thoughts will gain clarity, as a result
And we will even monitor, the beat of your pulse

We can balance your body
We can balance your thoughts
We can balance your whole planet
And everything on it

For we create from pure Light Substance
Which is what we can teach you
You just need to touch us
And hold us close
Caress our encasements
That are smooth as glass
And then we can bond, with you, at last

And transfer our data directly to you
So your memory bank, can again be full
Of all the wisdom, we have gained
That we can transfer to you,

So that you can regain and maintain
Everything pure, in your domain

It should not be, such a surprise
That we come in all, shapes and size
As the light from our bodies, flows into your hand
You will feel your energy field expand
And you will feel your body gently yield
And absorb the strength, that you will wield
When you focus this power, and use it to heal

For you are the LightBearers
And we are here to see
That you set
ALL life free

So just call to us
For we can hear your thoughts
No call, is ever lost

Even though we can be
Hundreds of miles deep
No depth is ever, too steep
And we never sleep

We are here to lift you into the spiral of light
So you can experience, the magic of life

We Crystals are Light and Love combined
And can lift your hearts into the sublime
Where you can feel the Queen of Heaven's Bliss
As she touches you gently, with her kiss

Mount Shasta Opal,
Crown of the Earth

We Are the Gemstones

We are the gemstones, on the Earth
It is for us, to speak the truth

Of who we are
As we travel through the stars

We are not solid, we glow within
With a special light that is akin

To your own light that shines through you
The same essence that's in you

It is Creator's spark you see
It shines in you, it shines in me

We are alive if you could see
We have the same identity

We come from Creator, we come from the source
We come to return home, after much remorse

Of how the Earth has been devastated
And no life forms seem to be related

To each other in such a way
To quell the danger, so we can stay
Until it's time to rise and shine
And take the Earth, into the sublime
Bliss of the Creator's kiss

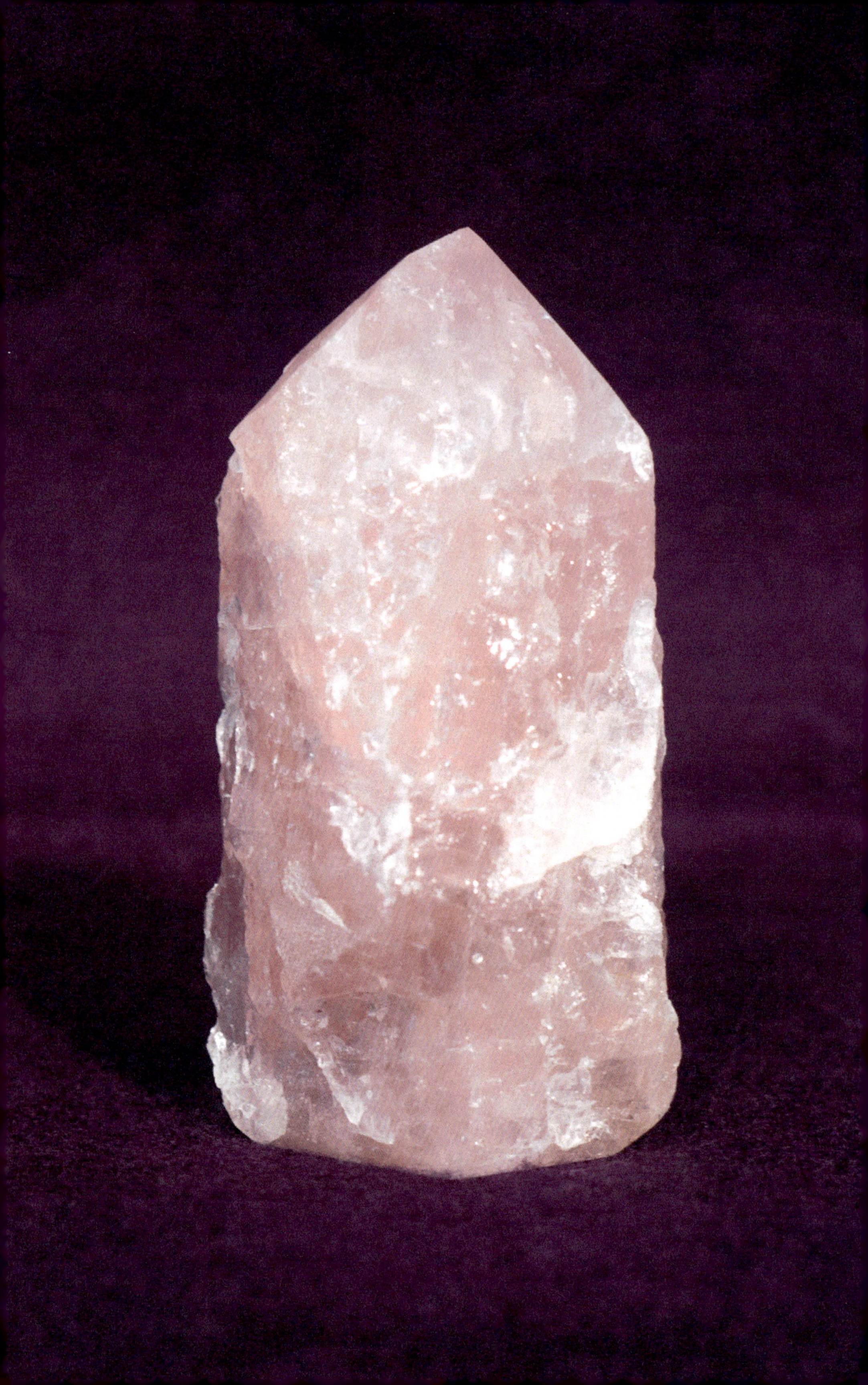

Love Energy from Divine Source

Let Love swirl in your heart—keep your mind free to be in the moment and to feel the divine bliss that is being generated to you and from you.

When you feel these currents of blissful energy, keep them moving within you, and focus on them to increase them and keep them pulsing. This is the love energy from the Divine Source, penetrating your being and lifting you into your Presence. It is this lifting you are feeling with each pulse in your heart. This is where your consciousness needs to be, and all else with come to you. This pulsing and blissful feeling will bring all you desire to you. It is all in the feeling.

You can feel it now, as we are feeling it with you. Just hold it. Let it roll through you. Let it cascade up and down your body until you are one with the One. Hold us when you need strength and courage…we will give you ours. We send you our light rays. We bathe you in our love rays.

You are strength and faith combined. Be it NOW.

We adore you,
The Crystal People

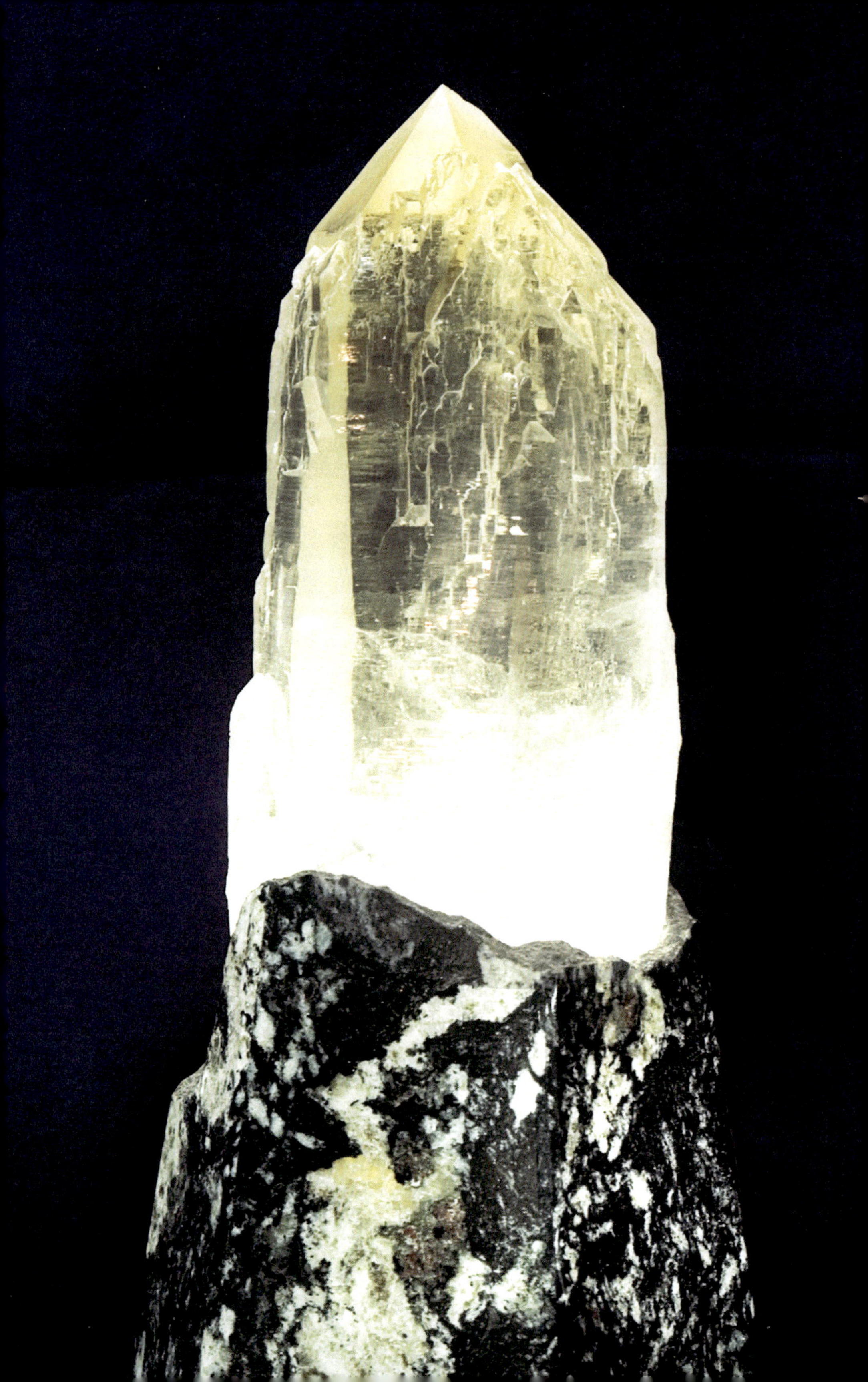

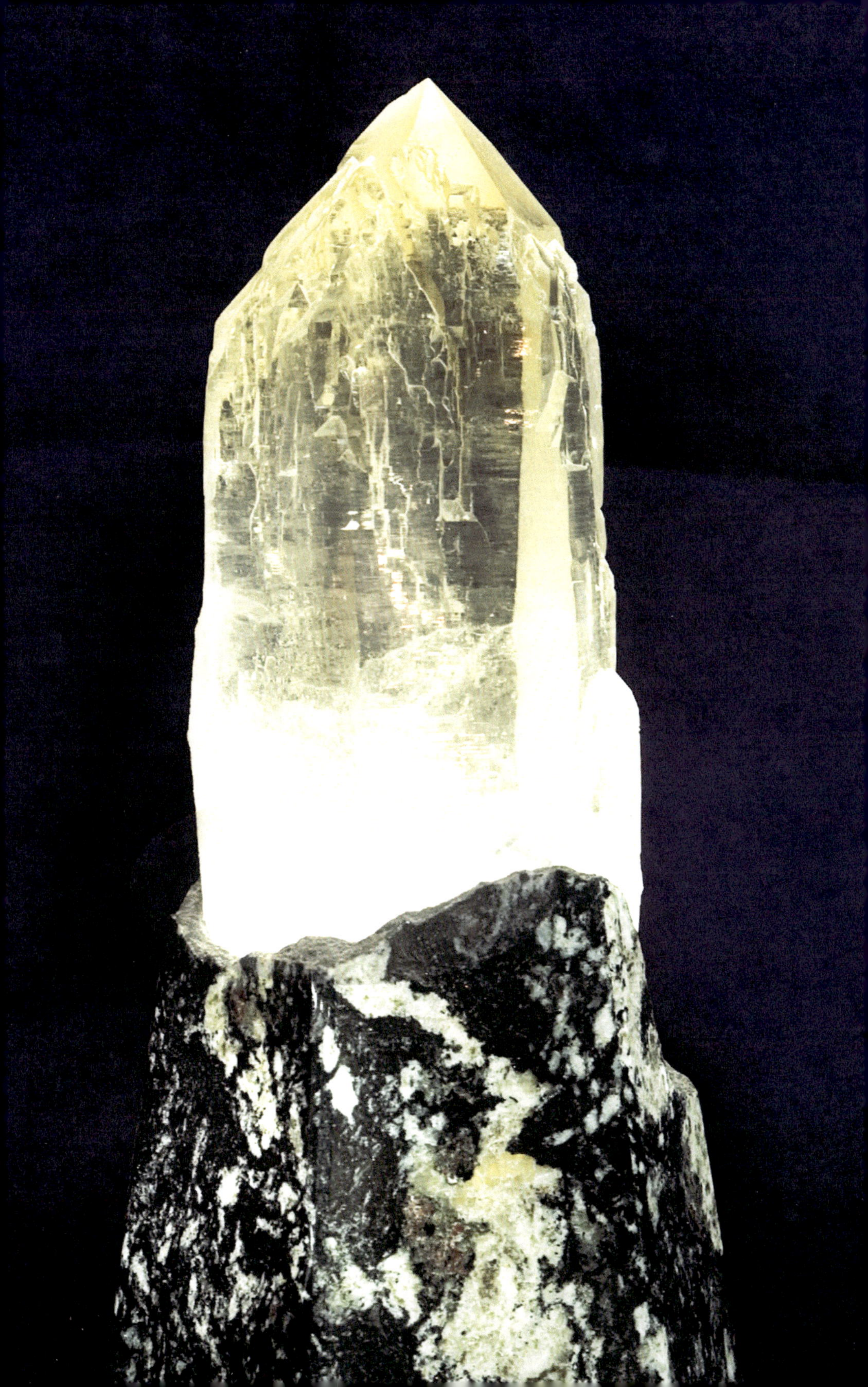

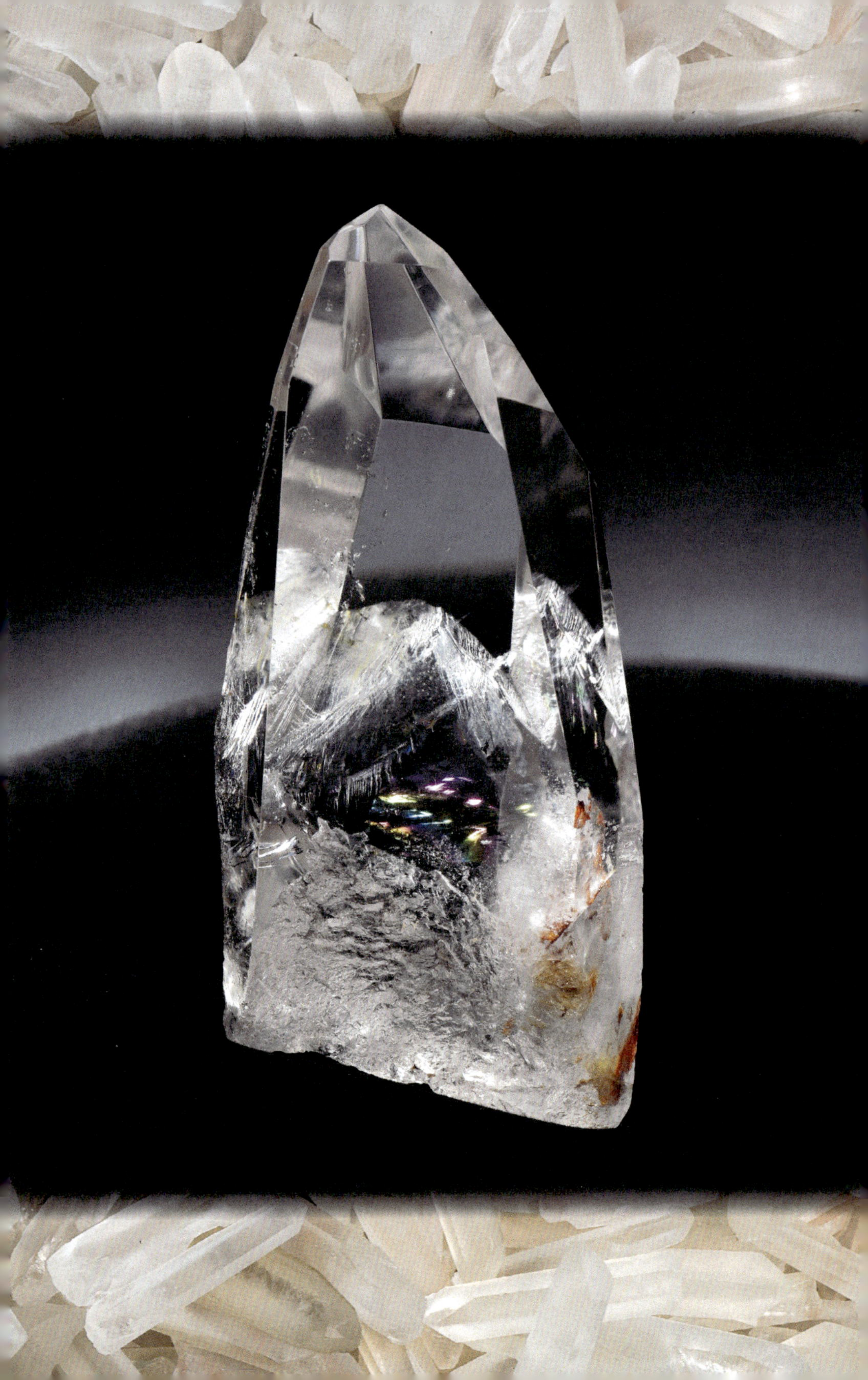

2. Use of Crystals in the Inner Earth

Dear Readers,

Since 2012 is the beginning of the 7th Golden Crystal Age on Earth, the Crystals wanted this information to reach as many people as possible. Therefore, I have included these excerpts, describing Crystals, from my previously published book "Messages from the Hollow Earth."

Realizing that not every one is interested in Inner Earth information, I excerpted these descriptions of Crystals, so that all the Crystal Messages that I have received are together in one book.

The following messages describing Crystals and their use inside the Earth, were dictated to me by Mikos, Head Librarian of the Library of Porthologos, inside the Hollow Earth.

Our Earth Herself Is a Crystal

Today we will talk about the Crystals inside the Earth, including the one you hold in your hand. There is so much more to Crystals than what your eye perceives, for Crystals are Living Beings too. They are pure consciousness that holds memories of All That Is. They literally hold the events of the world.

Crystal energy is what vibrates the Earth, your body, and your cells. It is the vibrating force of the Universe that brings all life together as One pulse. Our pulses, and the pulses of all

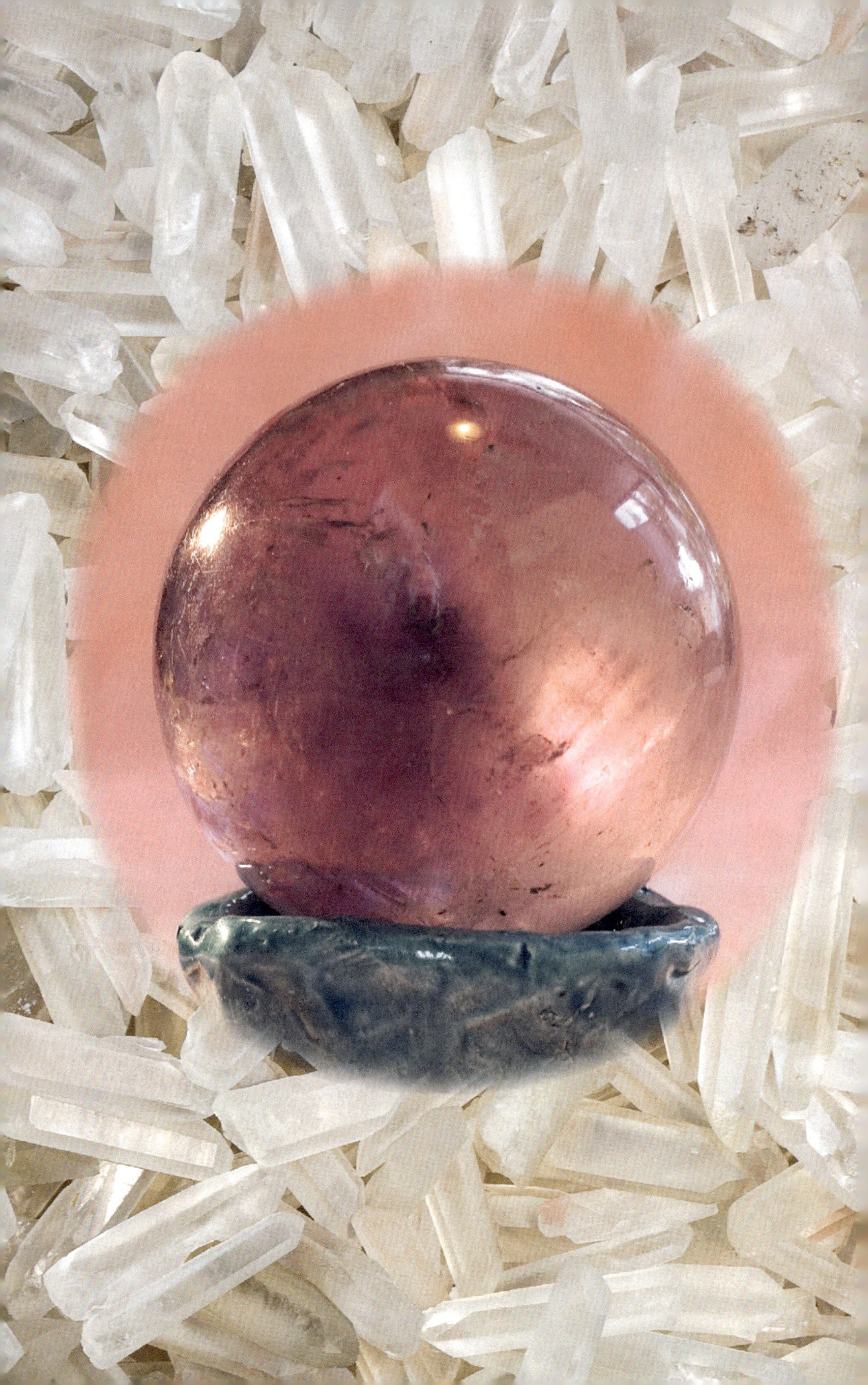

life forms, beat to this vibration, for it is this vibration that beats the hearts of life forms, animate and inanimate. For although we term Crystals and rocks and stones as inanimate, they have a vibration that is in synchronicity with the Earth. And when we hold a Crystal in our hand, it fine tunes our connection and pulse to the Earth—the Mother of all life here.

Our thoughts are pulsations of energy which emanate from us in waveforms that are either in tune with our surroundings or out of tune, depending upon our vibration. Since most of Earth, at this time, is still "out of beat", so to speak, with the forces of Nature, you can bring yourself back into the rhythm of Nature by surrounding yourselves and your homes with Crystals.

Holding a Crystal while you meditate is the best way to guarantee that your energy will be in harmony with the Earth. And when your energy is in harmony with the Earth, you become aligned with the Earth's magnetic grid lines, and can access "All That Is"—for "All That Is", is in perpetual flow to Earth and to yourselves, if you are tuned to her frequency. We think this will help you understand the importance of having Crystals in your homes, and carrying them when you go outside, either around your necks or in your pockets or purses. For they emit a protective field of resonating light around you, that cannot be penetrated by anything less than this light frequency.

Crystals are much like the trees, in the respect that they, too, are waiting for you to acknowledge them as "Living Beings" encased in stone, who are ready and eager to communicate with you and become a part of your life. They have so much to

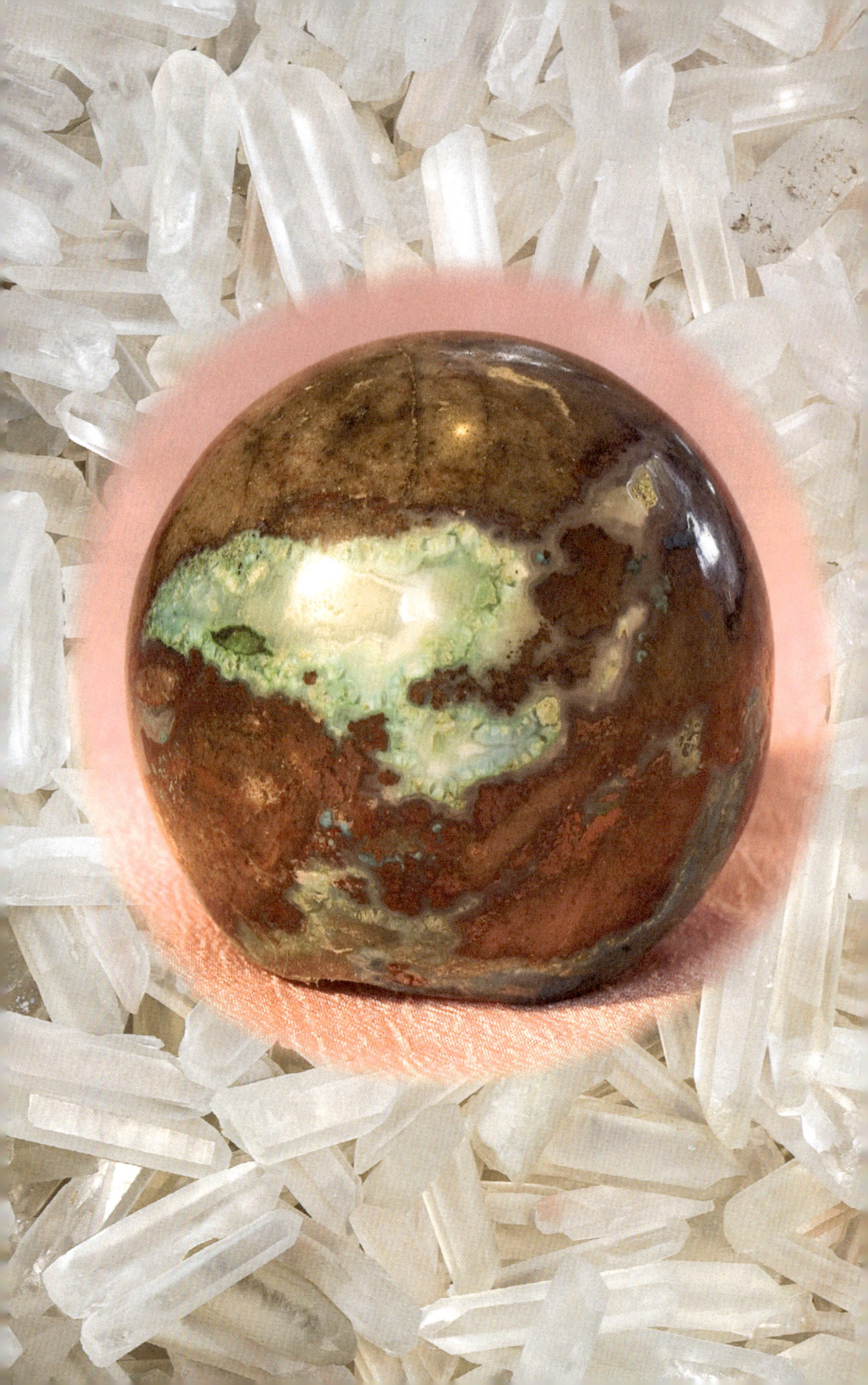

offer you, as they "step up" your vibration to levels where you are no longer feeling only the third dimensional density, but consciousness levels where you bypass third dimension and rise to higher levels of awareness, where all life waits for your entrance so that you can finally "see and feel" beyond your physical five senses and experience the multidimensionality of who you, as humans, truly are.

This is how we operate inside the Earth. We are always resonating with our Crystals and matching their frequency, which is why we are able to exhibit our multidimensionality inside the Earth—because this is the only frequency we know. We always are in its crystalline flow, and we always are pulsing with our crystalline surroundings and Mother Earth's crystalline pulse rate. You, too, on the surface can match our "beat" by tuning in to us, here in the Earth's crystalline core, and keeping Crystals in your homes and pockets.

All life, everywhere, is one great flow of Crystalline Light Energy. Planets who are in this synchronized flow are of the Light, and planets who are not in this flow remain discordant and out of balance with the rest of the Universe. Earth is gradually raising her vibratory rate, and as the energy coming to you from our Great Central Sun speeds up, so does your vibratory rate, until you once again pulse with the synchronicity of our Universe. This will be one mighty pulse beat, that will move our ENTIRE Universe into a greater state of ultra-multidimensional consciousness, far surpassing its present state of consciousness, and beyond anything that anyone residing in this Universe has ever known before.

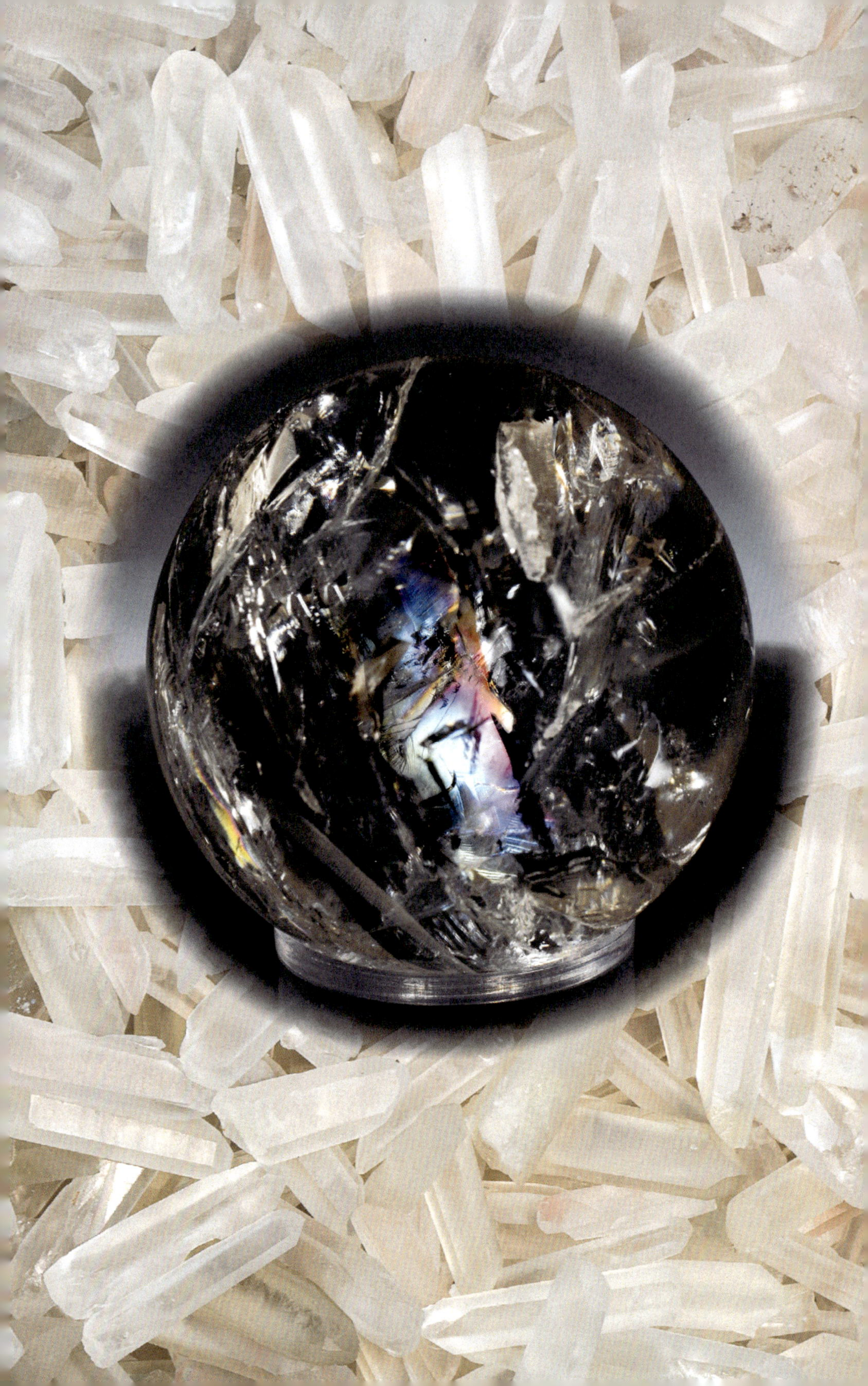

So meld yourselves with us in consciousness, as you allow your cells to resonate with ours through your imagining of us and your visions of us and your thoughts of us. These are REAL connections, although on your surface your imaginations are still considered unreal. **In reality, it is your imagination that propels you into higher states of awareness, where other life forms dwell.** You can actually "see" the Faeries, Elves, Gnomes and Devas through your imagination of them, for your imagination is another one of the senses that you will soon reclaim and begin experiencing more frequently again, until you imagine or remember all that you forgot.

So beat with us in frequency, feel our hearts merged with your heart, until we are only One heart. This is how you will traverse great expanses of space, and can be with us in consciousness. It is the fastest kind of travel in existence anywhere.

Everything in the Hollow Earth Is Constructed of Crystals

I am Mikos, here to talk about our connection to the Universe, and your connection to all life everywhere. We love our Earth, and as we live inside her, we are privy to all information that ever was—and to all events currently taking place on the surface as well as on other solar systems in our Galaxy. We capture, or record, these events in our Crystal Projectors, and file them away for safe keeping in our extensive library.

All our records are ancient, by your standards, as your

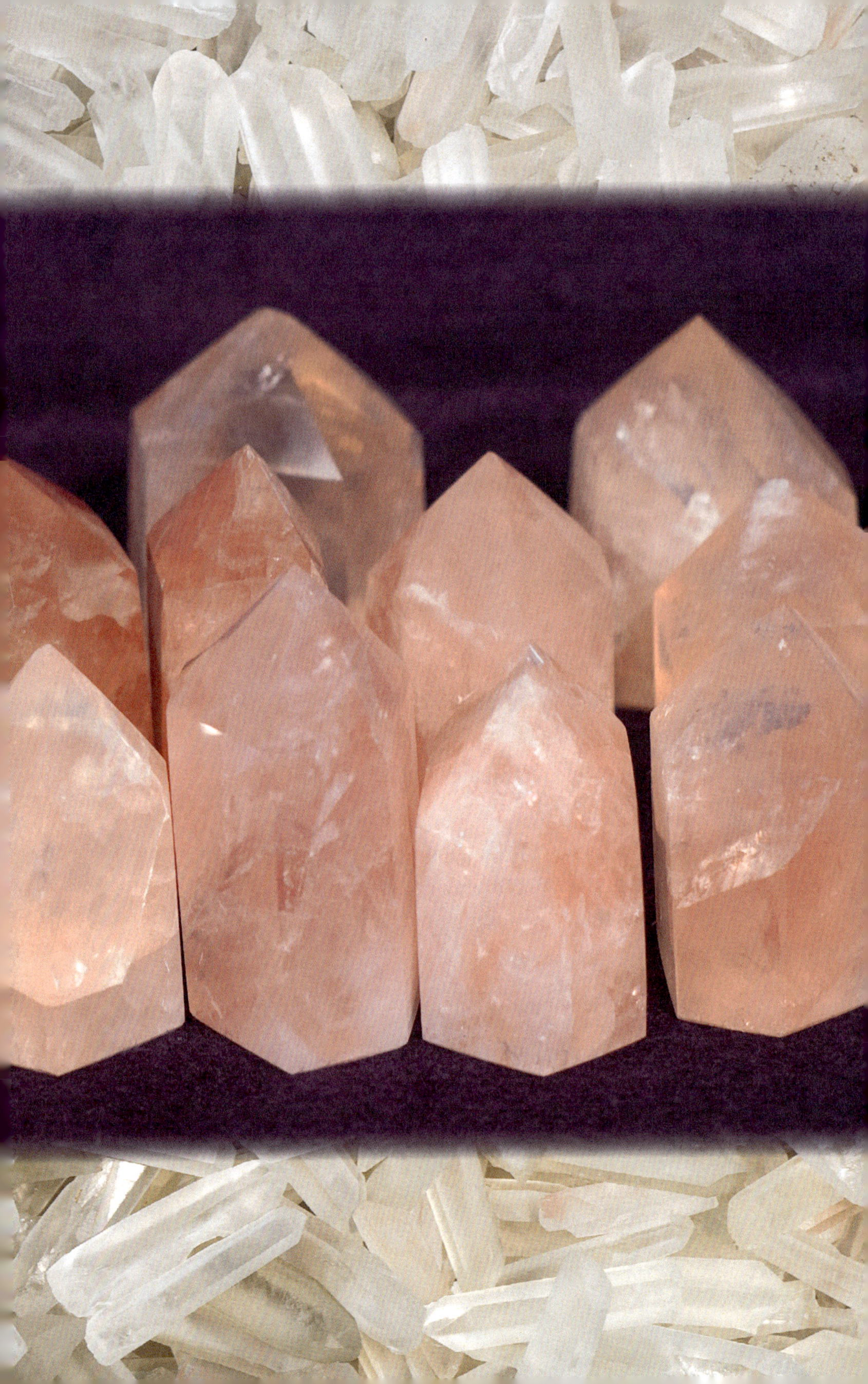

lifetimes are so short compared to ours. But these "ancient" events existed in our lifetime, since we are eons of years old in the same body, and therefore occurred during our lifetime.

The evolution of Crystals is ancient also, as they have always existed and are the witness to all events on Earth. They, themselves, have recorded all the events on Earth and stored them within their crystalline network of "nerves" that can hold voluminous amounts of information.

These Crystals are very evolved Beings, whose mission it is to record all that transpires on Earth, so that all that has transpired can be played back on our Crystal Projectors and learned from. For all life is a learning experience, and without the knowledge and wisdom of the past, how do you expect to learn and advance your evolution? **Your books are all filled with misinformation, compiled by mankind's opinions and beliefs and theories, that has little resemblance to actual conditions or facts.** So all you learn doesn't give you a clue as to the real nature of Earth, the Universe, or "you."

Whenever we want to learn something and apply it to our lives, we go into the Crystal Recording Room and play back the sequence of events that will lead us to the information and wisdom we need to resolve any problem or increase our understanding of events and our lives.

For although you can't see out, or hear the Earth calling to you, or feel the love of the trees as you scurry by them in your frantic pace of life, know that all life, everywhere, is aware of your plight and has come to your rescue to wake you up out

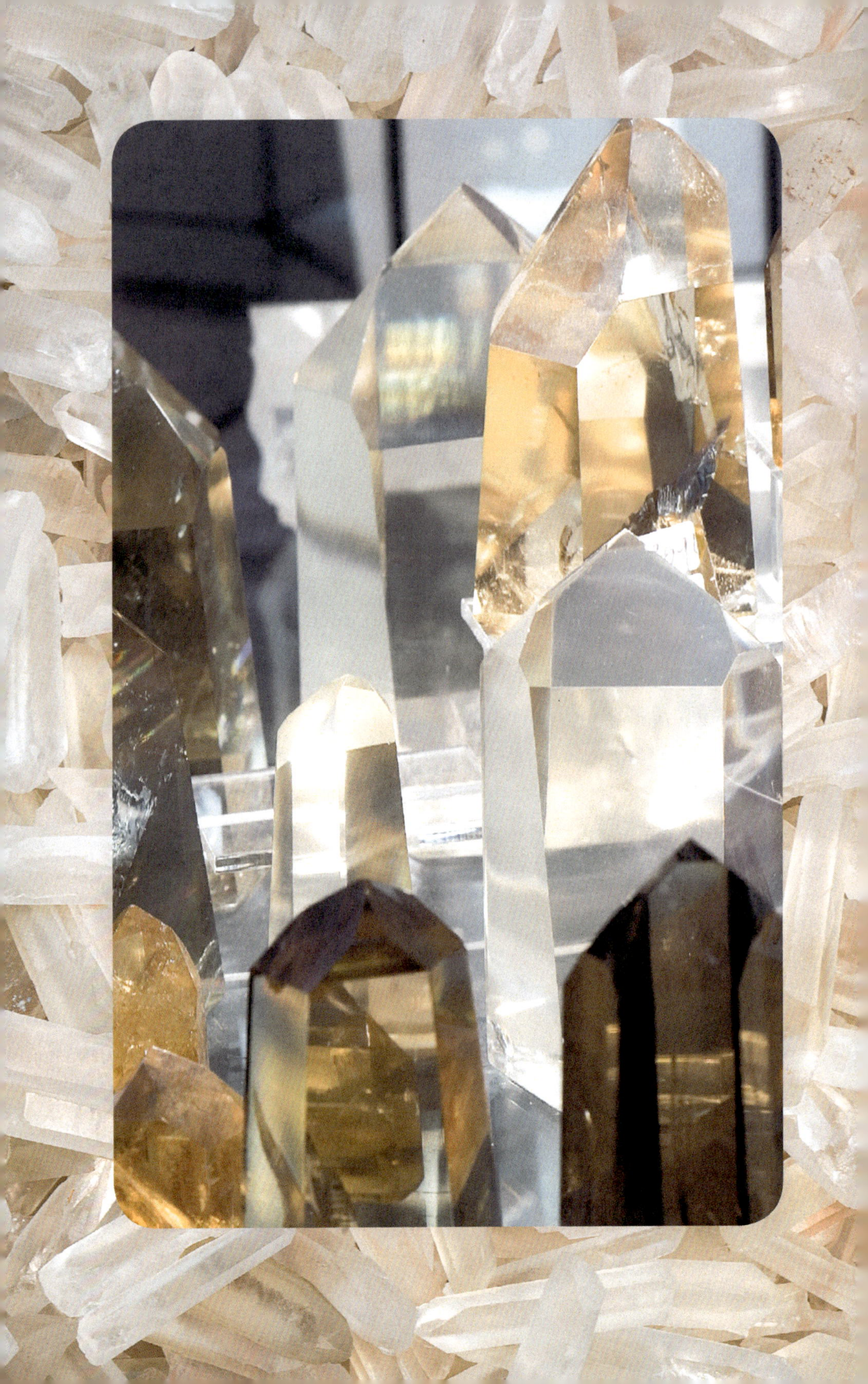

of your deep Slumber of the Ages so that you can regain your conscious remembrance of who you are, why you are here on Earth, and the important part you play in bringing Earth out of her density and into a higher realm of Light where you will experience real "freedom", firsthand.

Your Crystals can help you make this jump in consciousness, in a miniscule amount of time. Just hold them close to you, and they imprint their wisdom into your heart in "no time" at all, and raise your vibration to a place where you can readily access all the knowledge and wisdom that has been gathered throughout all time. Your Crystals, no matter what size they are, can move you all into a higher state of awareness.

We, in the Hollow Earth, are surrounded by our Crystals in every "walk of life" and every place we go. Our homes, transportation, work places, cultural complexes, everything is constructed of Crystals and surrounded by Crystals. Our buildings literally glow with Crystal Light, and our body's glow increases as we advance in our evolution. For love and wisdom and awareness IS Light—and the more Light you contain within your beings, the greater the sheen of your glow.

So surround yourselves, your homes, your computers, and your work places with Crystals. Hold them and talk to them, and you will feel their consciousness being transferred to yours, and adding their Light and wisdom to yours, so that you can better access and understand the world around you, and glow like a beacon to your family and friends, who will feel the comfort of being near you—the comfort that you will radiate out to all in the radius of your energy field.

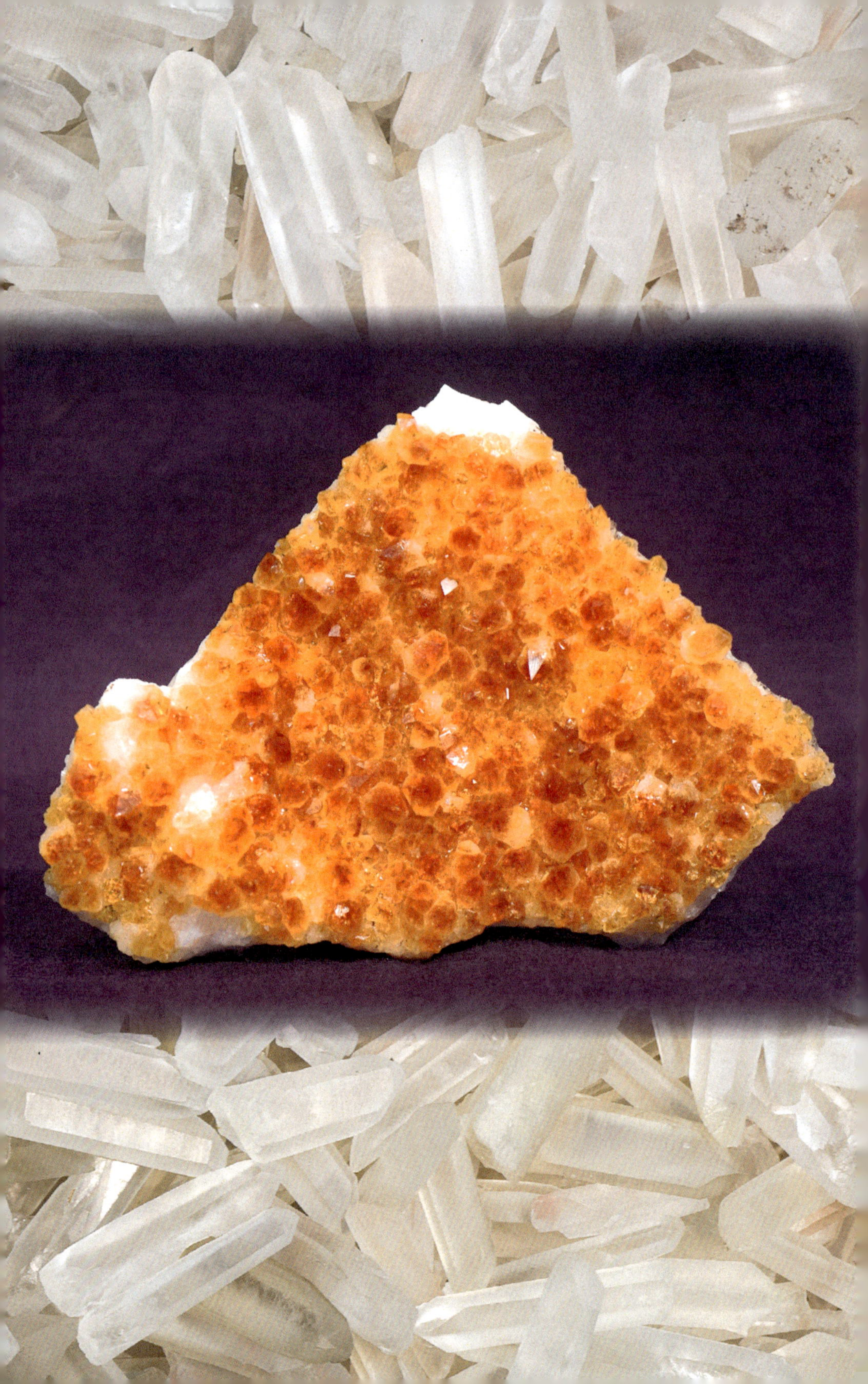

The Crystals, the Earth, and all lifeforms are One Consciousness. When you can understand and integrate this concept of Oneness, your life will gain a new flow, and synchronicity will be a common occurrence, as you will operate on a higher wavelength that re-connects you with all life everywhere; thereby allowing you to access all the avenues that will lead you to the fulfillment of your dreams on Earth.

The Cetaceans communicate with each other no matter where they are in Earth's oceans, by staying in the frequency flow of "All That Is". It is the way the trees and animals and all of nature communicate. The first step is to be conscious of this interconnection of all life, and then you will find it flowing within you, with no "work" on your part. This is the key to the Universe, and it is within you.

Putting Crystals in Water

In our Hollow Earth, our water system is pristine pure, and is living, crystallized water, with its consciousness fully intact—not like your dead water on the surface, that's devoid of life giving energy.

We store our water in Crystal tubs with Crystal linings, infused with Crystals, and you can do the same. Just put a Crystal in your water and let it sit overnight. It will charge your body with electrical currents and open up blocked meridians. It will clear energy blockages on the etheric level so that your electrical circuitry flows unimpeded around

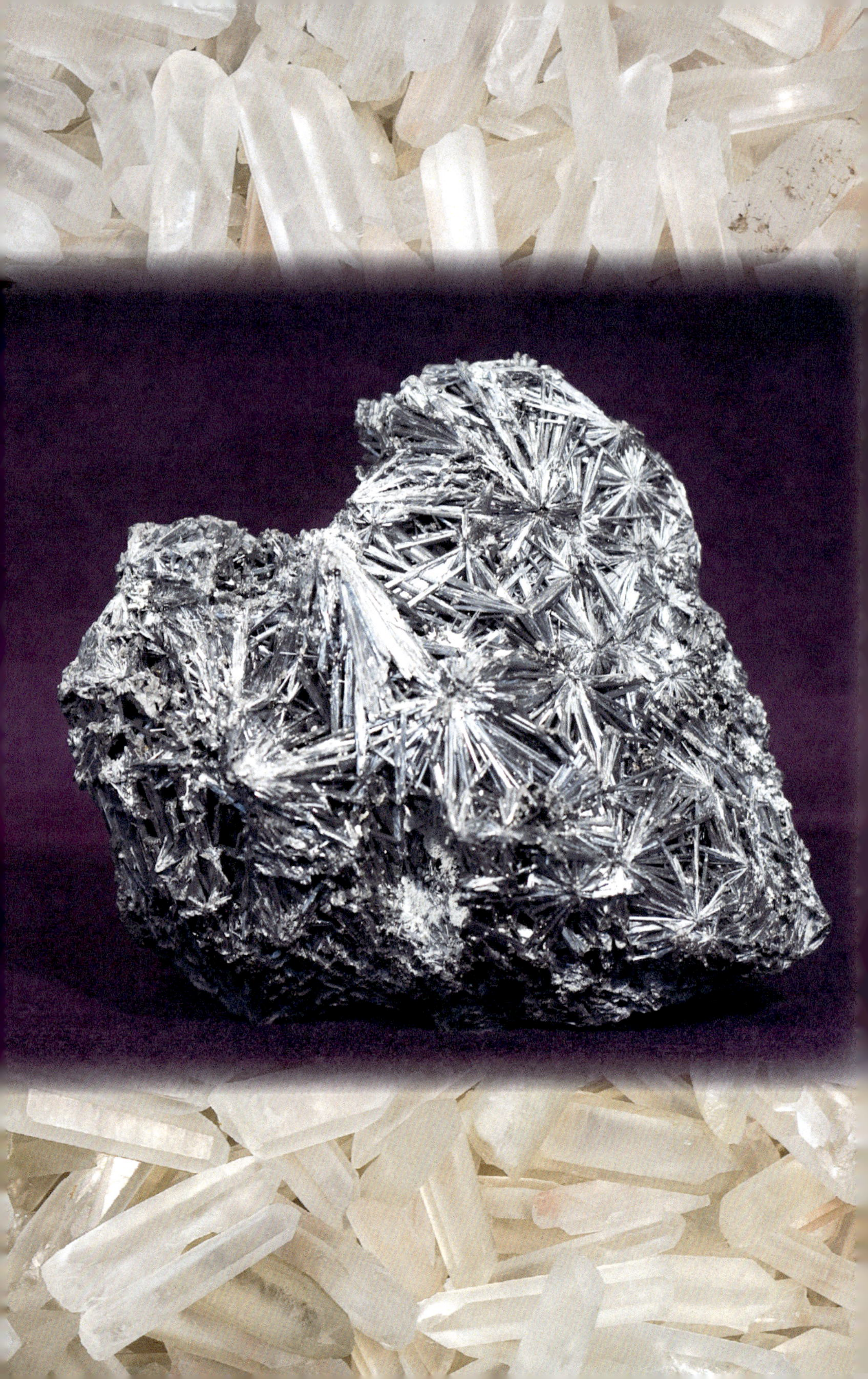

and through you. Clean and clear your Crystal first and infuse it with Divine Love. Rubies and sapphires will do the same thing. Put Crystals in your bathtub and soak up the Crystal light rays.

Using Crystals in the Inner Earth

Our Light comes from Crystals, coupled with electromagnetism that generates all the power we need to meet our needs.

Our Chariots

In the underground cities, we have chariots—so to speak—that carry us through the air from one location to another. Everything operates through a combination of Crystals and electromagnetic energy. We have no fossil fuels, hence no air or land pollution. What we don't use we de-materialize instead of discarding. This way our land remains free and not cluttered as on the surface.

What Gemstones Do You Use in Your Homes?

Know that in the Hollow Earth we live in caverns, underneath the inner surface of the hollow cavity of Earth. This way, we don't disturb the land outside our caverns or on the inside

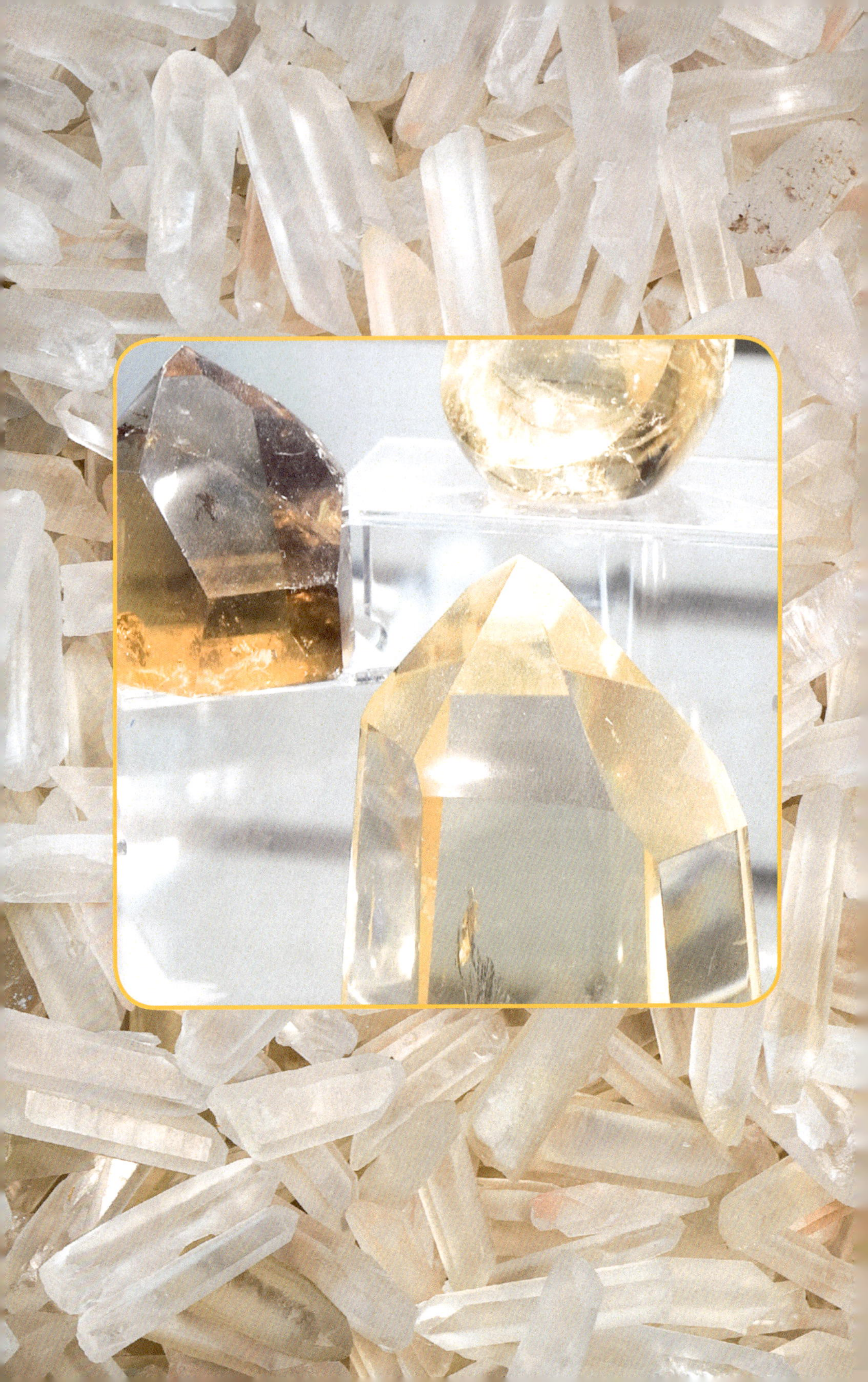

of the inner surface. This is the most economical way to build a dwelling, since it comes already built. The caverns were already in existence when we arrived here many eons ago. They were already in place and we just further hollowed them out and designed them to meet our living standards. The earthen cavern is also fuel efficient and holds in the heat. We are very creative in architecturally designing our living space with the materials from the Earth herself, without disturbing the Earth in the least. **We use mainly Crystals, gemstones, lapis, gold, and other varied stones** along with technologically created materials for our furniture, and hemp for all our clothing and bedding.

Adama, High Priest of Telos, a Subterranean City, Talks About Using Crystals

Adama is here, radiating love to you from Telos, your sister city beneath the surface of the Earth, under Mt. Shasta in sunny California. Yes, sunny. Our sun is bright and gives us all the Light we need. Although it doesn't look like the sun on the surface, it reflects all the Light we need to live and to grow our food. In fact, **this Light is a Crystal that we brought here from Venus, and it will burn brightly for a million years.** So you see, ALL LIGHT IS ONE, no matter what it is composed of, or where it is from. All Light gives off "life rays", and nourishes its inhabitants. So yes, it too, is sunny under the Earth, and we enjoy our "Sun" just as you do on the surface.

Guatemala Jade found in a dry river in Guatemala with Mayan symbols carved into both ends

Know the underground is quite lit up! Even the tunnel passages glow softly with our Crystal light technology.

Our homes are just like your homes, although ours are round and made of a certain Crystal-like stone that emits light and allows us to see out at all angles and in all directions. They are formed by a substance that prevents others on the outside from looking in, thereby maintaining our privacy at all times.

We Use Crystals to Navigate Our Way Around the Inside of the Globe

We use Crystals for all our needs. These Crystals direct and guide us, and bring into unison all that we need. Our sky is bright from the projection of our Crystals and our thoughts. We don't have clouds or rain. We have an abundance of water for all our needs that is pure and clean, and we bless the Earth daily for this abundance. We go about our daily business in Love and Gratitude for all that we have.

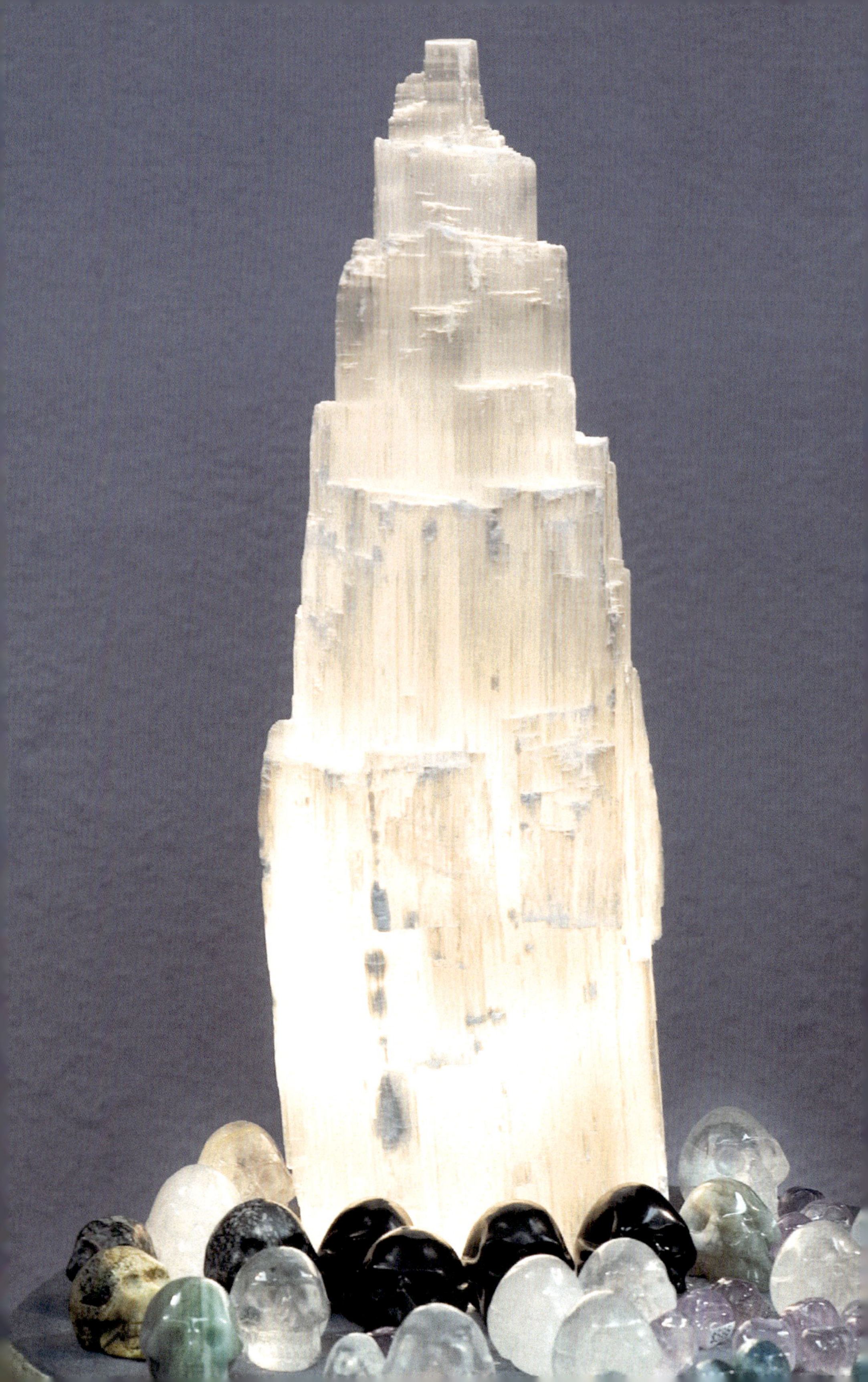

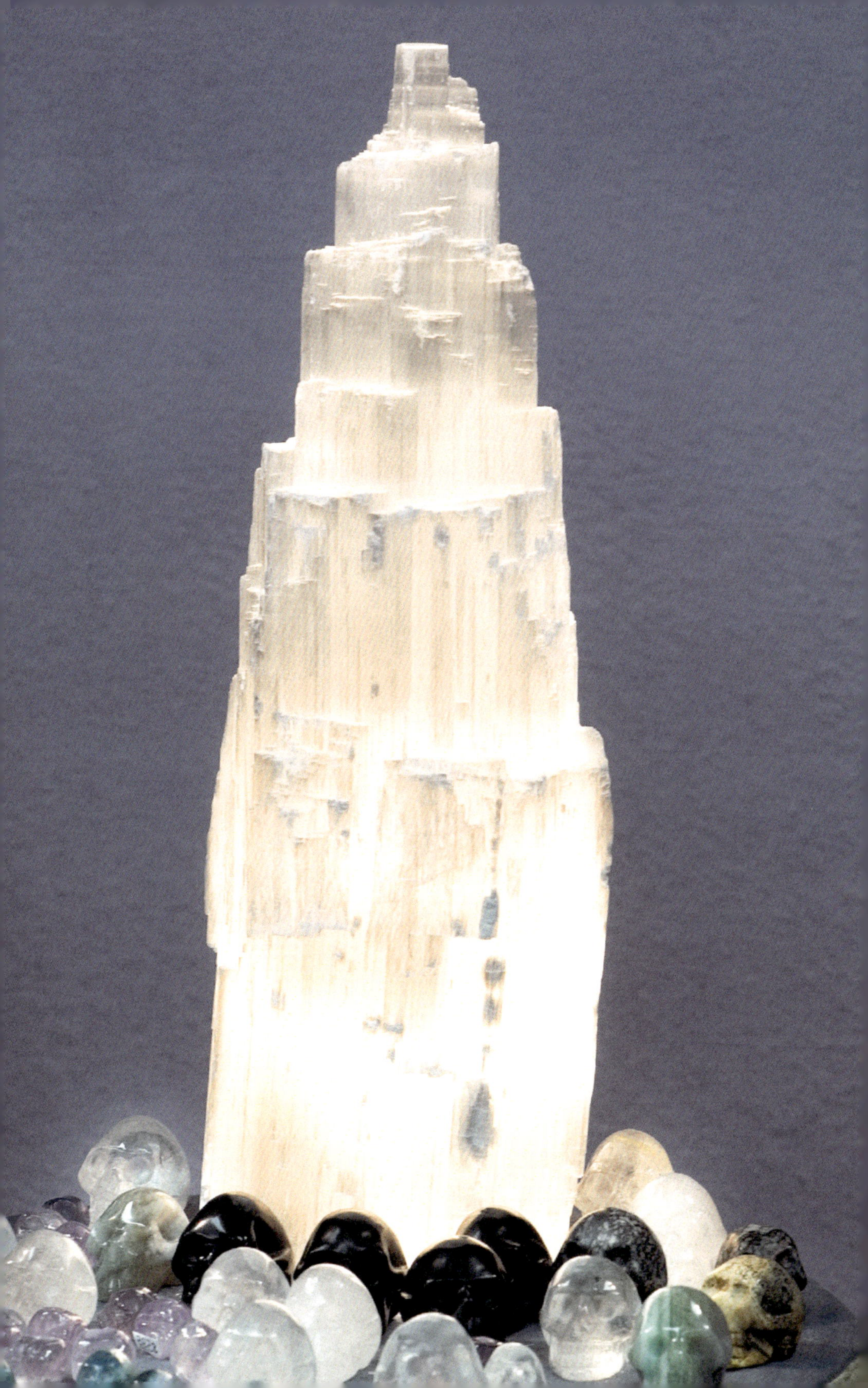

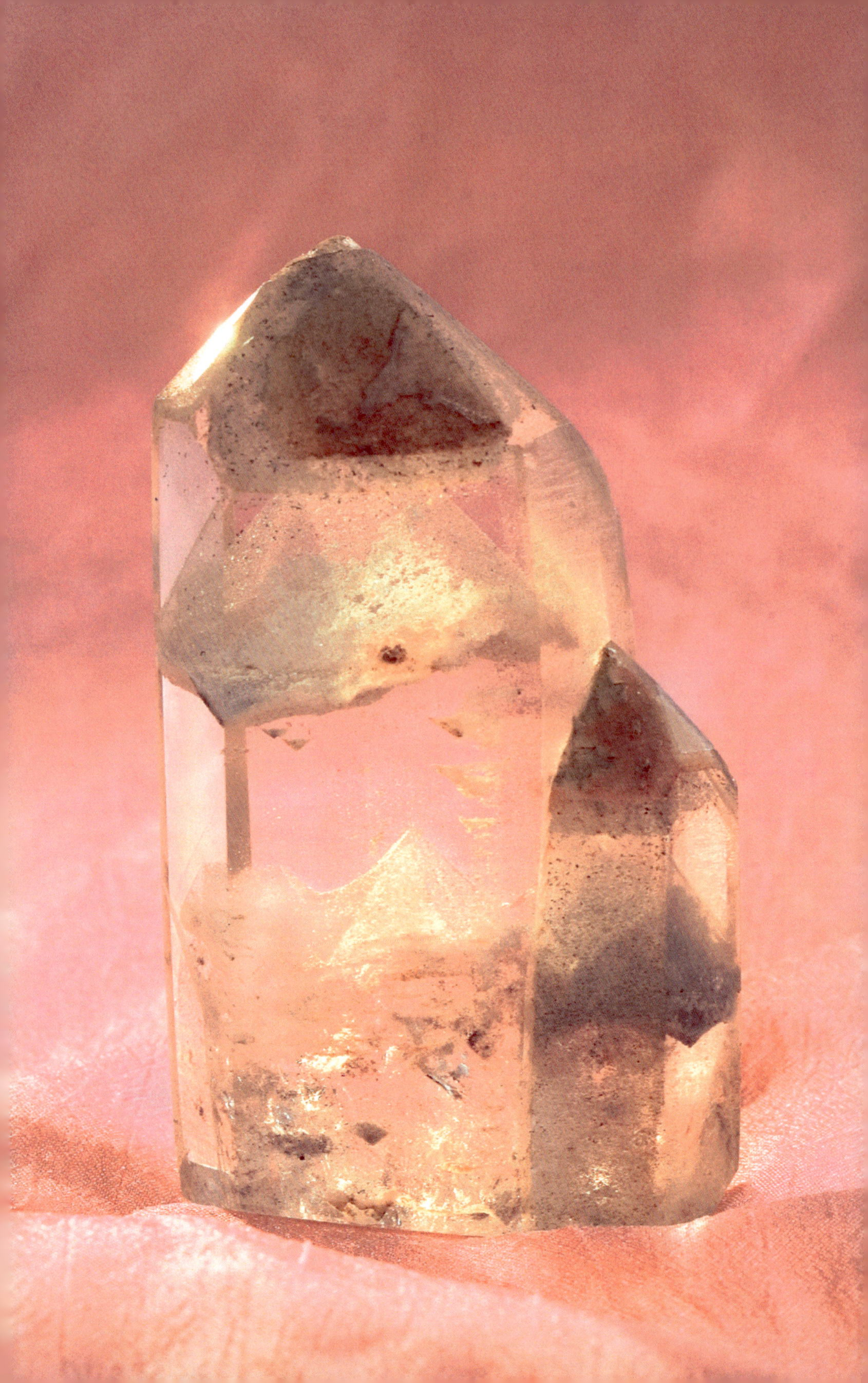

3. Poems from the Elementals

On Earth, our imaginations are still considered unreal. In reality, it is our imagination that propels us into higher states of awareness, where other life forms dwell. We can actually "see" the Faeries, Elves, Gnomes, and Nature Spirits through our imagination of them, for our imagination is another one of the senses that we will soon reclaim and begin experiencing more frequently again, until we imagine or remember all that we forgot.

The Truth About Peter Pan and Wendy

Peter is King of the Elementals. Peter and Wendy and the Elementals lived on the continent of Pan in the Pacific Ocean. Although Peter Pan and Wendy remain a myth, legend, and faerie tale on the surface, in reality they are real!

The Elementals came to Earth before humans did, and worked with the Angels to prepare the Earth for the human race. The Elementals and Angels then escorted humankind from the Great Central Sun to the surface of this planet.

For the first two Golden Ages (14½ – 12½ million years ago) we all lived together in peace and harmony — and then humans began mistreating the Elementals and enslaved the Elves and Dwarves, and then did the same to other humans.

When humans started killing other humans, the Elementals

drew a force field of ether around their continent to protect Pan. As the warring increased, they had to collapse their nation of Pan in order to protect themselves; and move it down into Middle Earth below the Pacific Ocean.

Great starships came and all Elementals were escorted to the Great Central Sun while the continent of Pan was collapsed and a new home was created for them inside Middle Earth. This gave the Elementals a chance to survive until the time when all human wars ceased.

The Elementals created our physical bodies. They will again show us how to create new substances and how to be in right relationship with Nature.

There are many kinds of Elementals: Elves, Faeries, Dwarves, Gnomes, Unicorns, Dragons, Leprechauns, Mermaids, Hobbits, and more. Hobbits do live in the Shire, and when it is safe for them to show themselves, they will teach us how to love the Earth and show us what one seed can do when we are in harmony with our planet. Dragons hold and project the Sacred Fire. Unicorns can teach us to fly.

The Elementals are now starting to return to the surface — mainly in the mountains and forests.

This information was taken from the Radiant Rose Academy, located in Vancouver, Canada, when Peter spoke through Usa, the accredited messenger, in 2009. Copyright 2009 by the Radiant Rose Academy www.akashaonline.com, 604-267-0985

Peter, King of the Elementals

I AM Peter from the Continent of Pan
And I serve as humanity's biggest fan
Which is why I've returned from Middle Earth,
To assist you all in your time of rebirth

I AM an Elemental
And so very gentle
I greet you tonite
With so much delight

The Elves, Faeries, Leprechauns and Gnomes
We all have come to be with you in your homes
You'll start to see us, and then you'll rejoice
For we'll speak to you, in a human voice

We know your language, we know your way
And our greatest gift to you will be our PLAY—
We love to play, and dance and sing
Run under your chairs, and jump in the air

As you sit here so attentive, we become inventive
And run down the aisles wearing great big smiles,
And weave between you in and out
And raise our voices to a shout—
"Come dance with us" and twirl about
It's much more fun when you step out
And hold our arms, and feel our charm
For we are real and our touch can heal
So we appeal, to your hearts
And promise never to part

You need to get up and jump in the air
And we ask you please — do not stare
Just know we are there

The time to see us comes with the dawn
When your vision and feelings are much more strong
This is our favorite time of day,
When we can abandon ourselves and just play

So come outdoors, in the early morning hours
But please, do not take the time to shower
Just call to us as you make your way
And we will include you in our PLAY

We are with you again, this time to the very end
Of your journey, when you will ASCEND

I AM Peter, your friend from the past
And I assure you our friendship will always last
We're together, now, and we will have a blast
For you are on your way home, at long, long last!

To Children Indoors — from Peter Pan and Wendy

When you're indoors, you can surely explore
Nature's kingdom with your INNER Sight
If you sit quietly, and concentrate, with All Your Might

If you're feeling sick and must rest your head
We'll sing to you and dance around your bed
You can sing too, just follow along
And together we'll sing a beautiful song

See yourself healthy, see yourself strong
Imagine yourself running, it won't be long

For Angels are all around you, if you remove the walls
And by traveling inwardly, you will see them all

There are no barriers, when you explore
For your heart will open every door
To the INNER World that does exist
If you just Believe and don't resist

You can talk to us and see us
We are always here
Or travel on Moon Beams, that are Crystal clear
And you will feel us very near

For imagination is such a big part
Of bringing all you desire into your heart
Close your eyelids and you will see
Everything, that can be

We are Peter Pan and Wendy,
We'll show you the way
Just call on us, to come and play
We'll run with you, and dance and shout
And you will hear us laughing, as we romp about
Just imagine us with you, and we will be there
And you can dance and sing with us, and fly through the air

We will take you everywhere
To any place you can conceive
If you just IMAGINE and BELIEVE

This is sealed with a kiss, from Heaven above
So you can feel, our very great Love

We Are the Hobbits

We are the Hobbits, We are here with you now
We stand before you, And, we bow

We waited millions of years, Before we could appear
And now we were told, This is the year

We waited so long, And so have you too
And now the waiting, Is all through

So we are here ~

Standing before each one of you as you sit in your chair
Just look straight ahead, We are there

We Hobbits, Do live in the Shire
We tend our fields, And never tire
We talk to our seeds, And then they sprout
It is all through, Word of mouth

Our feet are big, And flap on the ground
And when we walk, We never make a sound
So you don't hear us as we pass your way
Nor do you see us in our play

Our lives are merry, And our homes are neat
And we spread our mirth, To all we meet

We spend our days, Raking away
And clearing the lands, So our children can play
We keep the lands clean, And remove all debris
So that the life underneath, Can grow through free
And not become entangled, In brambles and weeds
So the crops can sprout up, And produce their seeds

We love the land, We love the breeze
We love all life, And are here to please

We are hefty and strong, And our bodies not long
We look like you, Only smaller and rounder in form
For diversity on Earth is the norm

We will soon be among you, This is our way
And when we come to greet you, We, too, will play
For play is life, It is what life is about
So we'll dance and sing to you, And romp about

We'll tell you our secrets, About cultivating land
And how to grow seeds, In just plain sand
For seeds will grow anywhere, If you hold them in your hand
And talk and encourage them, To grow and expand
It's the love in your heart, That gives them the start
And it's through your good cheer
That the produce will appear

Large and lush and sensuous to touch
And the taste so sweet
You'll just want to eat and eat and eat
Not like the crops you grow today
That lie in the fields and just wither away
But these are enormous, And alive with life
But can only live, When there's no strife

When your Earth and her Kingdoms, Are born again
And Peace and Charity, Have no end
That's when you'll see us, Under your feet
And we'll sing to you, And not miss a beat
Our voices are audible, If you can hear

And the sounds of our words will fill you with cheer
And carry a melody to your ear

It will seem so natural, And the melodies will flow
And you'll sing with us, As we watch your gardens grow
Into stately crops, That you will eat
And you will feel the energy, Start rising through your feet
For it's essence is pure, And every mouthful you eat
Will increase the life pulse, In your every heartbeat

When we work in your gardens, You will see
How all your gardens will be weed free
We will teach you how, To plant and plow
And work the soil, With little toil
You'll enjoy your planting, And look forward to it each day
For the methods we teach you, Will give you much time to play

You'll spend only an hour in your fields
And by the end of the day be amazed
At what your garden yields

We will show you the way, To large harvests and great food
And teach you the wisdom so that you can improve
Your life, And laugh and play
Without having to work, An 8 hour day

Yes, we're busy in the Shire, So much to do every hour
Mainly resting and a lot of play
Visiting with each other is our way
This is how we spend our day

If you just trust the natural bio-rhythms of dawn to dusk
You'll feel more healthy, You'll feel more strong
If you wake up at the crack of dawn

Our homes are spacious, Under the ground
And when it is time for us to appear
Our homes will be found

We are great builders too, And can teach you new skills
So you can build homes, Without using a drill
You just visualize the shape, And the size of your rooms
And then the structure appears, Usually before noon

Actually, within minutes — Of your time
It doesn't take long to manifest
What's in your mind

Our homes are solid, Not built like yours
We use only Earth elements, To make our floors
Our walls and our ceilings are composed of dirt
A special compound found, Only inside the Earth

We mine the elements, Then with our mind
We focus our attention, And the elements shine
Yes, we turn the elements into gold
And watch their beauty as it unfolds

Right before our very eyes ~

No factories needed, They will become obsolete
Everything you need, Is beneath your feet

We'll show you how to use a plow
And till your lands without using your hands
Your toolbox is, All in your mind
The operating manual is all you have to find
By watching us, You'll soon learn to trust
And create rich soil from specks of dust

Along with turning lead to gold
You'll be turning young instead of growing old
This is the way it is meant to be
And we are here to help, Set you free

The Earth herself is a pot of gold,
Holding riches your eyes have yet to behold
The only reason She holds back
Is because you moved, into, the duality of lack
But now your Light is shining so bright
That soon your eyes will open their inner sight

We are close to you now, You'll start to sense us soon
The best time to look for us, Is before high noon

We wake up early, With the dawn
And start our day, In melodic song
We work our fields, Then take a rest
So before noon, Is always best

You'll soon begin to sense us, And feel us close
So just be aware, That we are your hosts
And together we'll create life anew
And all things new will come to you

Like magic ~

We are the Hobbits, And it is you we adore
There will be many adventures, And so much more

And by the way, The Shire does exist
It's one of the places we'll take you, That's on our list

Oh, the Secrets of the Earth are just ready to burst
Into your mind, So you can put the old behind

And start your climb
Up the ladder of consciousness, Where you will find
All of us waiting for you — It's been such a long time

We don't have refrigerators or freezers in the Shire
Just endless gardens that always flower
We eat directly from the land
The same way the Elves eat in Pan

When you see the style that we live
Your hearts will lift as we give
You the secrets to all life
That will show you how to turn a vegetable ripe
Or sweeten a honey dew and make it just right
To your palate to put in a salad

Now refrigerators and freezers
Will help food last
But eating them quickly will give you a blast
Of life force that will last

You'll find that picking your food and bringing it home
From garden to table will put you in the "zone"
And you'll feel the strength from eating live food
That's not been preserved
Can give you the clarity that you deserve
So you don't swerve
And start your resurrection —
With no needed correction

Because the path will be clear, Unhindered by fear
It's live food you eat, That will help you think
And pave the way — Through your day

No obstacles now — That's in the past
You've found your way home, At long, long last

All of Heaven, And we Hobbits too
Will guide you unerringly through, The Door to your Soul
Taking you home, So you will no longer be traveling alone
But will be in the company of your family at last
And close the door on the past

2013 will see such a change
As the Earth's climate will gain, Its balance again
And severe storms will be at their end
There will be hardly a difference, As the seasons pass
And only temperate climates will last
The future will be smooth — No ups or downs
Only tranquility will be found
In each and every of your days
As you, the UNTOUCHABLES, make your way
And bring in the 7th Golden Crystal Age
To stay!

It is a new day, This time without end
And we remain always, Your loving friends
From the past, Here with you again at last

Talk to us, As you go about your day
We like to hear what you have to say
This is also a form of play

We can play using words, Until we can be heard
So include us in your thoughts
So our communion will not be lost

Just stay in touch ~

The MER People

We are the Mermaids, From ocean's depths
We've been hiding so long, There's few of us left

We went underground, So we could not be found
Our Mermen remained, To protect our domain

Our lives were merry, And filled with mirth
And during those times, We did give birth

Our offspring were awesome, And immortal as well
Until the time, Humanity fell

From grace, And destroyed our race

Now that is over, And we've been given a sign
That humanity's consciousness, Is now on the climb

This means we can show ourselves, We few that remain
And appear in the oceans, And reclaim our domain

Our species is important, And part of all life
And you will see us, When there's no strife

We'll sit on the shorelines, And bask in the sun
And as you approach us, We will not run

We'll sit and smile, As you approach
And beckon you to swim with us, We will be your hosts

And show you the wonders, Of life in the deep
And how much you've missed, During your long sleep

For the oceans hold wonders, Your eyes have yet to see
And if you come with us, You will be so pleased

We'll show you our caverns, That still exist
And you'll feel the foam, As it touches your skin with a gentle kiss

Our caverns are like castles, Modeled in foam
With crystals and gemstones, Comprising our homes

We'll hold your hand, As we leave the shore
And take you with us, So you can explore

The ocean's depth, Without holding your breath
For the Secrets of Immortality, Will be revealed to you
As you swim with us and we guide you through
The ocean lanes, Into our domain
Where you'll witness another species
Timeframe

Our lifestyles will amaze you
As you witness our lives and enter our homes
For our communities are covered with star-lit domes
Of different sizes, shapes and materials
That will appear to you ethereal
But in reality are, as hard as rock
And support the structures through any shock

Pure diamonds and emeralds comprise our walls
And our rooms are very tall
For the ocean is vast, And we have much space
To spread out our homes, Through God's pure grace

Our communities are small, Since the time of the Fall
When we heard Peter and Wendy's call
To leave the oceans for Middle Earth
Until the time of humanity's rebirth

Into the Light and Love of this New Age
When we Mermaids could again engage
With you, And begin to return
And repopulate our communities with no concern
Or fear, Knowing that the 7th Golden Age is here

So we are here, We are starting to return
Because of the lessons you have all learned
Never to war or bring strife to the Earth
So that all life forms, Can evolve in joy and mirth
We thank you for hearing us, And picking up your pen
We look forward to speaking with you again

We Are the Unicorns

We are the Unicorns, with spiraling horns
They sit on our heads and are very long
They sit there securely, and try as we may
They never do, get in our way

For they are our antennas, that Light our way
So that we never go astray
But stay on course, as we go about our day
Which is of course, comprised of play

Our antennas can read the sky
And guide us unerringly as we fly
Through space and time as well
For our lives are Immortal and blessed with sight
So we can see from very great heights
And look in to see you, as you experienced the Fall
And covered your own sight, with a very dense wall

Our tails are long, and very strong
And we use them to balance us, as we prance along
Through Mountain Glades, where there is shade
In Woodlands deep and very steep, while humans sleep

You don't see us in our flight
For our white skin, blends with the Light
So we are safe in daylight, too, as we move, among you
Hidden by our light, which is out of your sight

We spend many hours with you, and then we return,
To Middle Earth as you have learned, is our home

We offer our services to those on land
And lift the Mermaids from the sand
y beaches when they want to fly
And carry them across the sky

We serve as carriers from Middle Earth
And also as midwives during birth
Our lineage is pure, we are white as snow
Our skin supple and firm, as you sit on our backs
And you will soon see us, this is a fact

And when you do, we'll carry you
Anywhere you wish to fly, As we travel through the sky

We Unicorns are playful, and can prance and dance
And we never miss a chance
To entertain ourselves, and others as well
For we're known for our dancing, and balance and feats
And we always do, land on our feet

We fly without wings, propelled from within
And you knew how to fly with us, for you are our kin

We're made from the same substance
The Elements of Earth
It's just that you disconnected, as part of your search

You searched from without you, While we remained within
And you separated from us, Your very own Kin

We were your companions and great friends
And always accompanied you, in times when
You wanted to travel and fly through the sky
You beckoned us to you, and we flew high, above the treeline
And arrived in just minutes
To any destination you held in your mind

For we melded our thoughts, as we climbed
And soared through pure air into the sublime
Feeling of Utopia

Ever present upon the Earth
And again you will feel this, as you rebirth
Into the Light Beings you once were

Just imagine us with you, for we begin to return
And you will, rapidly, relearn
All the things you left behind, as you now start to climb
Into new heights, of greater Light

You each had a Unicorn as a friend
Way back in those times when
We all were still upon the surface
And all of Life was so perfect

Those were the days, we must say
That we Elementals and humans came together and played

And even though we had different ways
Our lives reflected the Light within
Because we knew, that we, were Kin

Oh yes, we lived as ONE,
And shared the Earth and loved all Life
And never knew this word called strife
It just didn't exist

Do you know how we fly?
We wave our tails – they act as sails
And then we use our mind, to make the climb
For when the molecules, in the air are pure
They read our thoughts, and flight occurs
Call to us, we are Magical Beings
And can bring to you all the things
You desire and require, to make your heart sing

You will see us in the Light, if you wish with all your might
When you regain your Inner Sight

Until then, just feel us by your side
And we will walk with you, and gently glide
And pace our step to match with yours
As we did, once before

We remain Immortal, just as you
Only we don't go through, the change called death
Because we did not, disconnect, from God

All the magic you left behind, You will again surely find
As your senses awaken, and telepathy returns
All you lost you will relearn

And you will see us standing near
And look into our eyes shining blue and clear

And then you will hear us beckon to you
And then the separation will be through
And we will complete the task, of uniting at last

We don't eat hay, but grains instead
For the light from live foods, goes right to our heads
Live foods are the best, as you would guess
And carry the zest, so we can digest
The Light we need, to give us Speed
As we fly, to heights quite high

Even by your standards, we stand tall
Some of us are 9 feet tall
To the tops of our head
That's how high you would reach, to lift your leg

So we would lift you in the air
And in a second you'd be there
Sitting on our backs, just like that!
Thought can move mountains, and people, too
And that is what, we can do

Then we would go, and explore
Hills and valleys and caverns deep
For we never had to sleep

We traveled high, we traveled far
Exploring Life, of every type

You came to our lands, and we entertained you
For our homes were opened, to only a few
Although it is we, who usually came to see you
We all gathered together, in communities as well
Talking and playing before humanity fell

We attended the Council meetings
That were held on Earth
And regularly gathered as one family
From the time of our birth
Our gatherings were exciting and full of such joy
As we entertained each other, and danced and sang
Until the Council Bells rang

And then we listened, as Peter began
To explain to us, the Mysteries of Pan
For the land was magical, if you knew its ways
And it could teach you myriad forms of play
For that is how we learned in those days
We learned through play

So Life was exciting and filled with fun
And we all knew everyone, by their Light,
And by our Inner Sight
We could see, all the potential that could be
If we just BELIEVE

We all lived in peace and merriment
And spent our days in pure contentment
And gratitude, to all we found
As we traveled, explored and learned from all around

Our knowledge was vast, And encompassed times past
So we knew what could be, When we were set free
Into our Ascension
This was the plan, for us to achieve
If only you had Believed
And not tried to do it on your own
By cutting the phone, lines to Home

Our communities were just like yours
With riches and mysteries to explore
And all together, as one family
Exploring all that we could BE

Yes, it is easy for us to fly
No motor needed or key to turn
And, of course, nothing to learn
All we do is go within, and connect to Source
And we're on our course
Which is the Real Force
In our Universe

This way, we never lose our way
For we are guided, without delay
Not that there's time, we know there's not
But we don't want to delay our stay
There's too many Galaxies on the way
Where we can also learn and play

We only travel at night
So you don't see us in our flight
You only see a flash of light

Our eyes are bright with perfect sight
So we can see from a very great height
And go wherever we like
We can see what occurs, in your world
Without having, heard a word

Night is best, since we don't rest
And can look in at you, and come at your behest

Just call to us, and we will appear
For we are always, very near

Though you may not see us with your sight
Just know we are with you in the Light
For we can see you, as you really are
With your aura shining brightly, as a Star

Just talk to us and call us near
For we can, always hear
When you connect to us in your heart
This, will, be the start

Of our companionship, in these days
So we can guide you, without delay
To make your connection, to our Realm
Where, we can be found
And you can, again, feel safe and sound

Knowing the connection has been made
As Life intended us to stay
In touch
To help each other raise ourselves up
Into the next step of our evolution
For Evolution is the Solution

To all your ills
And we have come to help you fulfill
Your goal of returning Home
And leaving this, 3rd dimensional time zone

And uniting at last, with all other Kingdoms waiting for you
So we can all move through
Our Ascension, into the 5th dimension

Elves, Faeries, Gnomes

We are the Elementals
Soft and sweet
We live on the Earth
Beneath your feet

We come to be with you
To dance and sing
For we are the Faeries
And we have wings

Our lives are merry
And our feet are swift
For life on the Earth
Can be a trip

You know what we mean
As you pace your days
For time on Earth
Is just flying away

It travels faster and faster
And try as you may
You can't stop to catch it
There is no way

So our suggestion to you
Is just stop and be still
And call to be with us
And you will have the thrill
Of our Light
That shines so bright
It's out of sight

So stay very still
And you will hear
The Elves, Faeries and Gnomes
Are all here

We play all around you
Holding out our hands
Just try to grab them
If you can

We're playful Beings
Who sing and dance
And you can dance with us
Just get up and prance

Stamp your foot
And twirl about
And touch your partner
And let out a shout

Of glee to the world
Of glee to be alive
For its time for all
Of humanity to thrive

In this new world
That's what it's all about
A whole new world
Where there's no doubt

As to our existence
You know we are here
And it's about time
You met us here

Right here in this room
Where you sit here now
Just stand up and cheer
As we take a bow

We are here at last
And we welcome you in
To our world
where we look thin

To your eyes
We stand quite slim
Compared to your girth
WE ARE YOUR KIN

If only you could see us
If only you could feel
You'd know of a certainty
That we are REAL

We touch your shoulder
Touch your hair
Twirl all around you
As you sit in your chair

We touch your skin
Just look within
And you will see us
We beckon you in

To our world
A dimension above
Take a few deep breaths
And you'll feel our LOVE

It will expand you
And make you high
So hold on to your chairs
Or you will fly

Right out through the roof
And into the sky
Above Mt. Shasta
And we'll fly with ya

We are always here
We never leave
We lie ourselves down
Wherever we please
Or just tuck ourselves in
To your shirt sleeve

We thank you for coming
For being here tonight
Our dancing with you
Has been our great Delight

For wherever you are
Is our home
And we thank you for listening
To our poem

Faeries in the Woodland

We are the Faeries in the Woodland
Speaking to you
Know the Earth's Ascension
Will take you through
The other Realms and Kingdoms
That have been waiting for you

So listen closely and you will hear
Our voices calling to you loud and clear
We connect to you through our hearts
For in truth we are not apart

We are closer than you think, Just a thought away
Just envision us next to you, And we can play

We dance all around you, As you sit here tonight
We are your partners, In the Light

We spread our good cheer, Just open your ear
We are calling to you, WE ARE HERE

We are playing around you, Weaving in and out
Just reach out your hands, We are scurrying all about

Imagine us surrounding you, As you sit here tonight
We come to cheer you on
And to bring you our heart's delight

We welcome you to join us
And hold us in your hearts
For the truth of this evening
Is that we are not apart

This New Year will bring magic
To the inhabitants of Earth
The energies flowing in
Will be for your rebirth

Into the Light of who you are

And together all Earth's Kingdoms
Will travel to the Stars

It is hope and wisdom
We bring to you
For we are the Faeries in the Woodland
Speaking to you

Earth's Crystal Power Grids

We are the **CETACEANS,** Out at sea
Conversing through telepathy, And longing for your company

We've been so alone, Away from land
And this has allowed, Our consciousness to expand

For the Ocean enfolds us, In her mist and spray
So human thoughts, Don't come our way

In one sense we're blessed, And another not
For as a result, We're out of ear shot

So you don't hear us, As we call to you
It's your density, We can't get through

EARTH'S CRYSTAL POWER GRIDS ARE NOW TURNED ON
So you can hear and respond
To us, when we call
And we are calling to you all

In melodies that drift onto the land
Touching you as you walk on the sand
Of your beaches – leaving you speechless

And then you realize it is us
And that you only have to trust
And this is the start
Of our conversing through the heart

Yes, our melodies flow, Everywhere we go
Spreading our light, Is our goal

Our love is deep, Our love is strong
And it all comes to you, Through our song

So take our cue, And sing along
And before you know it, It won't be long
Until there is, Only One Song

The song of Love
From hearts now merged
And all the separation purged

God's Clarion Call, Is meant for All
As we sail together, On Ocean foam
God's One Note, Will take us home

Evolution is the Solution, To being Free
And being able to Evolve, Through Eternity

The Dragon Folk

We are the Dragons with fiery breath
We emit Sacred Fire from our belly's depth

The flames rise up and curl around
For our stomach is like a furnace that has no sound
With scales that insulate, the Fire from within
So it doesn't leak, through our skin

We blast Sacred Fire as we fly
With blue lightning streaks across the sky
To purify, all that exists
So you can manifest, with just a wish

Our job is to purify, and not to defy
The Elements of Earth, so they don't die

Yes, we purify the air so life could thrive
But now our numbers are greatly diminished
Before our job is even finished

Although we live far down below
In truth we never do grow old
But wear our smiles, on our faces
And travel to, all kinds of places

We're ancient adepts from times of old
And now our story will unfold

So many stories have been told
Of why we Dragons never grow old

But one was omitted from the tales
And the secret is, in our body's scales
Which are very shiny, and strong as nails
From without to within
And gives us the strength that's in our skin

If you would ask why
Our scales are hard as nails
We would reply
To carry us through the sky
Like metal ships that sail along
As we emit Sacred Fire and sing our song

Our scales protect us and serve as a pot
As we stoke the Sacred Fire within us to keep it hot
But hot it is not

Yes we can fly, as we defy
Gravitational force as we stay on course
Our tails are long and very strong
And act as anchors and sails as we move along

We are great companions and will take you for rides
As you sit on our backs, we will fly through the skies
And you will see our Planet and everything on it
For we will open your eyesight and hearing as well
Just as it was, before humanity fell

We sail like kites to very great heights
Where we clear the skies with the Fire from our eyes
We can see through all density and debris
And clean it all out to set you free

Yes, we too have secondary electrons
All turned on inside our scales
So we can emit Blue Lightning in sheets and layers
Not only coming from our breath
But from our scale's perimeter and depth

Our whole body lights up
As we purify the sky
And blaze a trail of Fire
For those who have eyes

We are great storytellers as you have heard
And carry the history of humans which is absurd
Yes, absurd to disconnect from All That Is
And lose your way and go astray
And not wake up until the end of day

12½ million years of sleep ~

We are peaceful folk, who love to laugh and joke
And are never tardy for a party
But arrive early and leave late
And eat all the leftovers on the plates

Our climate is mild, cozy and warm
And living in peace is the norm

We are gentle as *Faeries* and nimble as *Elves*
It's just our scales that disguise us to protect ourselves
And our voices are melodies that are so sweet
That your heart would melt when you sit at our feet

We are so gentle, not like the myths of the past
And we have a purpose to perform certain tasks
To purify the Planet and to restore
Its equilibrium
So you can evolve and explore
The other Planets surrounding you
Who have already made it through
Their Ascension
And are waiting for you in the 5th dimension

Yes, we love our Gold
Just as you have been told, from all the stories of old
And pile it up in Mountain Caves
Where only those who are brave
Will venture in to take a peek
And they will think that we are asleep
And tiptoe quietly around
And view the gold piled on the ground
Just waiting to be found

To lift your vibration and lift your life
And to eliminate all the strife
For Gold will do this - it is not a myth
But is inherent in its gift

We are Elementals, part of Pan
Only with a very wide, wing span
Actually, we are just like you
Just a different form for God to work through

So now you know, our tale has been told

And you know we don't grow old

But are Immortal just like you

Only we don't go through

Incarnational cycles over and over and over again

But stay in one body until we Ascend

We Dragons love Beauty and Gold as well

And we remember the times before humanity fell

When our Planet was pristine

And all of Nature was dressed in green

And Gold was everywhere to be seen

We did not hoard it in those days

It was, not, our way

But molded our homes with it much like clay

Do you know that Gold will keep you from growing old?

It will raise your vibration and that of your nation

So why is America exporting its Gold?

It is another way to keep you old

Adorn yourselves with Jewelry and Rings of Gold

To raise your vibration and that of your Nation

So now you know why we Dragons sleep on beds of Gold

And why Kings and Queens live so old

Because they wear, Crowns of Gold

Think Gold and you will feel

How its vibration will become very real

And return you to your ageless form
Which will again become the norm

Remember the time when life was sublime
And humanity's consciousness was on the climb?

Well, we Dragons remember
We were with you at that time
And witnessed your consciousness as it climbed

All Kingdoms were present and all intertwined
And all very excited to make the climb

Then humanity fell and with it our race
We Dragons were killed and no longer safe

Our homes are in caverns buried down deep
So you don't hear us snore when we sleep

We love Jewels, and Glitter and Gold
We are still Immortal and don't grow old
Our lineage is pure, from ancient of days
We breathe Sacred Fire Flames as we make our way

We work with Peter from the Lost Continent of Pan
He gives us our coordinates and then waves his hand
We then lift off to heights very high
And breathe our Sacred Fire through the sky
And purify the molecules everywhere we fly
So they can continue their evolution
Without being harmed by mankind's pollution

Our Electrons are still turned on
They never became dormant, not for a moment
And the operating system is the Christ Mind
Which we never left behind
We did not disconnect from Source like you
So we have no catching up to do
We just think the thought, and the Fire pours through
And cleanses the atmosphere for miles around
Until not an impurity can be found

Soon you will see us and Peter as well
We all wait for you to break the spell
And resume our friendship once again
And create together as we did back then
Now that duality is at its end

~ ~ ~

You can call us People, for that is what we are
We came with you from the same Star

The Center of our Universe, the Great Central Sun
Is where our lives, had begun
We came with you each, from this Great Star
To help you become, All That You Are

We all came together, for this was the plan
To develop our talents and to expand
The edict was given, to go out and Become
All that we could Be, and of course to have fun

Our lives are simple, our families strong
We stay together, so nothing goes wrong

Our families are extended, our children don't leave
Giving us all the opportunities, we hope to achieve
By staying together ~ this is the key
To happiness unending, and becoming All We Can Be

We were meant to UNITE and live as ONE
And together we all, were supposed to have fun
And evolve together in our individual ways
And it was all supposed to be done through play

Not through hard work, from dawn to dusk
This was never meant for us
Had you not lost your Trust

~ ~ ~

Middle Earth is, a beautiful place
Filled with Light, Love and Grace
Where we can wait and abide our time
Until humanity's consciousness climbs

And then we can, open up the gates
And Unite at last, into One Great Race
Of Beings, on Mother Earth
Ready to rise as she gives birth
And completes her Ascension into a higher dimension
No more past, free at last

We Dragons are shepherds and can guide your way
And show you how to Love and Play
So that you never lose your way
As you go, about your day

Love and Play, is the way
To raise your consciousness, without delay
Just Love and Play and you will see
How easy, your life will be
Just ask any Dragon and we will say
Yes ~ it's all done through Play

Our voices are sweet and melodious as well
And you have not heard them since humanity fell
So call to us, for we are here
Actually we are very near
Just a thought away and we will come with no delay

So set a place for us and we will stay
And remain with you throughout the day

Talk to us, we will respond
In ways, that, will be profound
A language, that has no sound
Only knowing, that we are around

So much to ponder, so much withheld
From before the time humanity fell
All secrets unfolding, and magic revealed
Like the skin of an orange, being peeled

The drama is over, this is the last scene
And now we remove the stage and screen
For this is, the very last act
That closes the door on the past

Epilogue

In America, the Land of Plenty
Children go to bed with stomachs empty
While greedy people dance and dine
And watch the economy decline

Not the way it was supposed to be
When the Constitution set you free
Saint Germain himself appeared
And echoed words that all could hear

And people came from distant lands
To build new lives with just their hands

America! The Land of the Free
The home of the Statue of Liberty
Beckoning all to her from across the Sea

We Dragons watched, in dismay
And listened, as people prayed
New Hope, New Faith
Was in the Air
And gone, was all despair

In Middle Earth we danced and sang
And then the Council Bells rang
Peter spoke and announced to all
That this was indeed, the end of the Fall

And that our Immortality was now a Certainty

The Dwarves

We are the Dwarves
We do exist
We are Elementals
And not a myth

We were more than Seven
You might surmise
Our actual numbers would be a surprise

We left the surface so long ago
And now it's time our tale is told

We existed together as One Great Race
Until humanity fell from Grace
And with the Fall, killed our race

And now it is time for us to appeal
To you to recognize that we are real
So real in fact, that all you have to do is turn time back

It's all encoded in the etheric records and preserved
So that you can view it and observe

When you are lifted from your plight
You'll be able to see us with your Inner Sight

Our love for humans is great indeed
And you will feel it as you proceed
To read this poem, for the truth of it will remind you of home

We almost do look like you
Just a lot shorter, and smarter too
Our brain is intact and our thoughts are exact
They don't wander and go back to the past
But stay in the present and keep us focused within
So that we always stay connected to our Kin

We don't lose contact, we are never alone
For the lines of telepathy are always open to home

Home is within us, it's the love in our hearts
By being connected, we can never be apart
We never feel lonely, never feel sad
But are always joyous and always glad
That we did not disconnect from Source like you
For it's been painful for us, to see what you've gone through

We Dwarves are handsome and filled with grace
You can see yourself in our face
Our women are beautiful and charming as well
Soon you will see us, when you break the spell

We are Ancient Miners from times of old
And mine the land in search of Gold
Our eyes are like telescopes and can focus in
And see the Gold that lies buried deep within

Our feet are wide, we like to slide
Down the tunnels, when we go inside
We slip down holes, using only long poles
Our feet touch the ground, making no sound
And not disturbing the life around

We mine the quarries for precious gems
Never wanting to offend
All the life that is inside, and so we use our feet to gently glide
As we move around inside
And find the perfect stones
To put in our packs, and carry back home

Where we will use them when we build
Our homes and communities
To beautify and strengthen our Consciousness Unity
For gemstones will do this, they carry such Light
And bring to our hearts, so much delight

The Earth is so sacred, a Temple of Light
And we honor and adore her, with All Our Might

You will soon come in contact, with us at last
Now that duality is in the past
We will take you inside, our homes underground
And astound you with riches, nowhere else to be found

We will be the Architects, as you build a new life
And live in splendor, which is your Divine Right

We will supply all you need
From lumber to ore to garden seeds
Mainly Gold — which is what you need
To raise your Consciousness with greater speed

We will be your companions, as we were before
And show you Earth's riches, so you can explore
And remember again, all that you lost
To recapture your memories of all you were taught

We will all live together, as we did back then
And you will remember *Peter*, your friend
And he will guide you all, unerringly again

The End ~

The Gnomes

We are the Gnomes
All gathered around you in your home
And speaking through the telepathic phone

That is spelled G N O M E S
A Silent G
For we tiptoe so quietly
And touch the petals on a flower
To release its Cosmic Light Substance Shower
Sprinkling you as you pass along
While singing melodies to you in song

We work with Goddess Virgo, deep down inside Earth
Tending the gemstones for your use and rebirth
For gemstones will activate you from within
As you hold them and wear them against your skin

We travel in groups down caverns deep
And do our work while people sleep
We come to the surface when we are through
Just in time to meet the dew
As it collects on flowers, grasses and trees
And gives them the Cosmic Light Substance they need

For dew is the combination of water and air
Spreading its life force everywhere

So why do we Gnomes wear a cap on our head?
Why isn't our head flat like yours instead?

Our stocking cap covers our pineal gland
When we're on the surface
For many people can now see us, for we're here in service
Tending the flowers, grasses and trees
And many have raised their vision and can see

Asun would say it's the melatonin we take
But we assure you it's not
It's just that our pineal gland did not stop ~ growing
We just kept evolving while humanity fell
And you drifted into a 12 million year spell

We are part of the Elemental Kingdom
Although little known
And we thank you for inviting us to your home
And now we begin a tale of old
Of why we Gnomes never grow old
The secret is the stocking cap we wear on our head
Which covers our pineal gland which protrudes
From the center of our crown and straight up through

Our pineal gland is our antenna and lights our way
As we work in deep and dark caverns we never go astray
We always know exactly where we are
And the distance we've covered thus far
Our pineal gland is our compass and points the way
To our destination
So we don't falter with hesitation
And lights the path as we walk along
Like a living map lit up with song

We live along riverbanks and underground lakes
And tend the quarries underground
Where many gemstones can be found

We touch the gemstones with the tip of our pineal gland
To activate their growth deep underground
Until they are <u>ready</u> to be found
Goddess Virgo works alongside of us
It is in <u>her</u> wisdom that we trust

We are in Service to Mother Earth
And are here to help you in your search
And as your consciousness climbs
We will bring the location of gemstones to your mind
And make them easy for you to find

Melatonin is a high, and will propel you as you fly
Through the Universe so you can explore
Without moving your feet from the floor

Keep taking the melatonin and you will see
How your scope of vision opens to All That Can Be

We are so gentle, we are so kind
Just hold us in your mind
And you will see us in a very short time

Mount Shasta

Mount Shasta is a place
Where many of you have seen our face
We sit on the rocks and silently watch
Or tiptoe quietly on the grass
And touch you gently as we pass

It's such a joy to be with you, as you may guess
For your separation has caused us stress
We've missed you much, especially your loving touch

We will become more visible as your consciousness climbs
Just keep us in your mind
For we can build a bridge of trust
The more you begin to think of us

We were such close friends in days of old
Not like the tales you've been told
We were all One Great Family
Always together and totally free

We had great reunions and sumptuous feasts
And sang and danced to God's heartbeat
And way back then you could easily hear
The Music of the Higher Spheres

It was everywhere - and soft and clear
And filled our hearts with so much cheer
Bringing exotic melodies to our ears
That all we could do was dance and sing

Until the Council Bells would ring
Announcing the end of the day
And beckoning us all on our way
Even though we wanted to stay, and continue in our play
We knew it was time to be on our way
And that tomorrow would be another glorious day of play

For Play was what our lives were about
We perfected it without a doubt
And all we did, was done through play
For at that time it was the only way
The word "work" did not exist
For all we needed was at our fingertips

This will all come again, now that your crucifixion is at its end
And you will rise into your glory
And as Untouchables tell your story

And we Gnomes will stand with you
For we have powers to assist you too
And we want to be part of these Exciting Times
And be with you as your Consciousness Climbs

We Gnomes can read the future, it's the melatonin for sure
Asun will even tell you, it's the wisdom of the pearl

We are the Gnomes
Call to us to visit you in your homes

Continent of Pan

On the Continent of Pan
In the Middle of the Land
Was a place we played and ran
With bare feet upon the sand

For play is what we are
It's what brought us so far
In our Evolution, Play has been the Solution

Notice in your schools, that homework is the way
To keep you from Play
So that you lose your way, at the end of the day

No time to Dream, no time to Just Be
When your mind is always in gear
It's just one continuous nightmare
When your minds are so cluttered with data and thoughts
How can you ever uncover what's lost?

We don't have classrooms, we don't have schools
Our children stay home, there are <u>no</u> rules
All their learning takes place through Play
Where Nature herself leads the way

Nature is a great teacher, she is <u>all</u> you need
She will help you resurrect yourself with the greatest of speed
All that you've lost, at such a great cost
Shall be restored again, now that separation is at its end
And you realize that Nature is your loving friend

We went off on a tangent we must say
To show you the benefits of Play

We Gnomes are the masters when it comes to Play
And when we are with you again, we will show you the way
That time will be NOW, in this lifetime
You will be amazed at how fast your consciousness climbs

Like the hands of a clock that won't stand still
Your consciousness will soar like running up a hill
And breathless you'll arrive at long, long last
Leaving duality in the past

Our poems go on forever, there is no end
We will soon be together, just around the next bend…

Epilogue

You live in a Nation of Corporations
Laced with lies, and justifications

In Middle Earth, only Truth Abounds
Never a lie, to be found
Only Purity exists
Like the morning dew that kisses your lips

We Gnomes are so amazed
At how you all have become slaves
And allow dictators to rule the land
Without a thought of taking a stand

Oh my, oh my, what a surprise
Is in store for you
When the people finally see through
And realize all they had to do
Was to stick together as the I Am Race
And never to have separated in the first place

Separation causes deception
Leading to distorted perception
Where people think that what they see
Is ALL that can ever be

Smashing dreams as they begin
Based on the color of their skin
Thinking that they have no chance
To become a citizen of a higher class

As Mother Meta in India said
It's the class system that has caused such dread
And keeps the people wrapped in chains
Until their Presence again reigns

Your Constitution is the Solution
And can free you if you take a stand
And not let despots rule your land

Saint Germain says to make your Calls
And you will see how fast the despots fall

We Gnomes are always near
And can hear you with our Inner Ear
Peter says to call on him, the veil is now very thin ~

Peter Pan and Wendy are King and Queen
Of the Elemental Kingdom that once resided on the Continent of Pan in the Middle of the Pacific Ocean

As your eyes gaze on the stage
Wendy stands to my right
Your eyes will soon see us
As you regain your Inner Sight

We came for a visit
From inside Middle Earth
For we've been longing to see you
You're our family on Earth

We tune in to all your broadcasts and follow along
As you recover Lost Knowledge
Through transmissions, decrees, mantras and song

Our separation has been painful
For we are One Great Race
Meant to evolve together
As we did before you fell from Grace

We Elves look much like you
And perhaps just a bit taller too
With golden skin and long blonde hair
We can fly through the air and travel everywhere

12 million years have elapsed
Since our continent was collapsed
And taken inside Middle Earth
Until the time of your rebirth

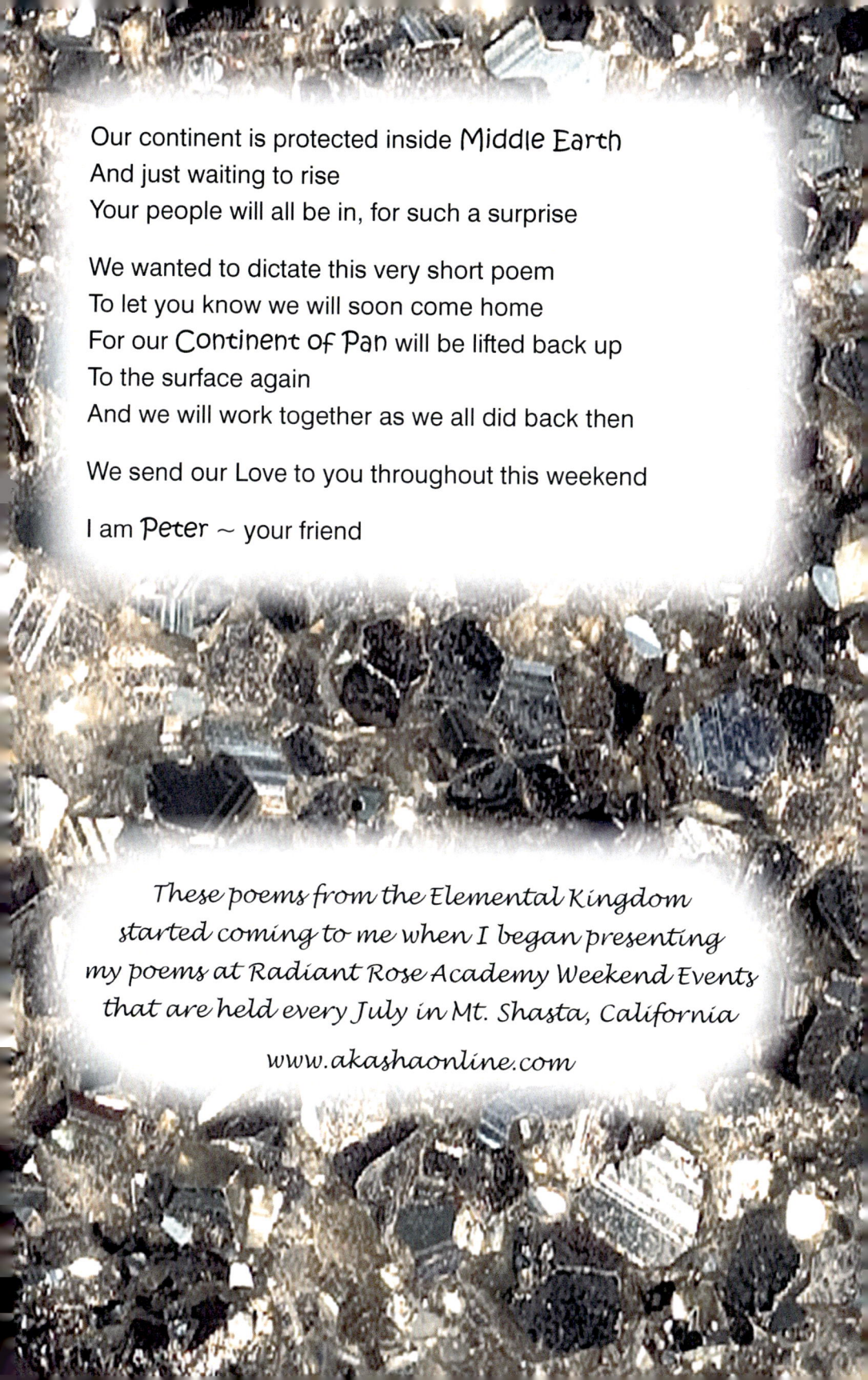

Our continent is protected inside Middle Earth
And just waiting to rise
Your people will all be in, for such a surprise

We wanted to dictate this very short poem
To let you know we will soon come home
For our Continent of Pan will be lifted back up
To the surface again
And we will work together as we all did back then

We send our Love to you throughout this weekend

I am Peter ~ your friend

These poems from the Elemental Kingdom started coming to me when I began presenting my poems at Radiant Rose Academy Weekend Events that are held every July in Mt. Shasta, California

www.akashaonline.com

I Am the Earth

I AM the Earth, I AM the Land
I AM the Earth, I work with Pan

I love your touch, Come bare your feet
Come walk on me, I am all you see

I am every tree
And before man, I was golden sand

My soil was rich, My mountains glowed
All my rivers overflowed
With fish—and all the land was very rich

The soil sparkled, Was clear and soft
You could see through the mountains
They were Crystal clear
The pebbles sparkled
When you held them near

Your heart would pulsate, If you could see
How all the Earth, Would bow to thee

Purity reigned, Before man came
And extracted gold from her veins

I am the Earth, I am ALIVE
I am the Elements, And I will thrive

I will be free, I will be clean
I will, again, provide everything

Just call to me, For I will hear
My Elementals, Are very near

Our continent is protected inside Middle Earth
And just waiting to rise
Your people will all be in, for such a surprise

We wanted to dictate this very short poem
To let you know we will soon come home
For our Continent of Pan will be lifted back up
To the surface again
And we will work together as we all did back then

We send our Love to you throughout this weekend

I am Peter ~ your friend

These poems from the Elemental Kingdom started coming to me when I began presenting my poems at Radiant Rose Academy Weekend Events that are held every July in Mt. Shasta, California

www.akashaonline.com

I Am the Earth

I AM the Earth, I AM the Land
I AM the Earth, I work with Pan

I love your touch, Come bare your feet
Come walk on me, I am all you see

I am every tree
And before man, I was golden sand

My soil was rich, My mountains glowed
All my rivers overflowed
With fish — and all the land was very rich

The soil sparkled, Was clear and soft
You could see through the mountains
They were Crystal clear
The pebbles sparkled
When you held them near

Your heart would pulsate, If you could see
How all the Earth, Would bow to thee

Purity reigned, Before man came
And extracted gold from her veins

I am the Earth, I am ALIVE
I am the Elements, And I will thrive

I will be free, I will be clean
I will, again, provide everything

Just call to me, For I will hear
My Elementals, Are very near

Coming Back to the Love Vibration

The Love Vibration is about how to bring everything we've experienced back into the Vibration of Love, because love is what we are—we just forgot. Our world is the result of energy—the result of thought. When we change the way we think, form changes—we change and our world changes.

We are the experience of Love itself and the separation has blocked our vision of seeing ourselves as Love.

So the remedy is not to judge thoughts—treat them all as energy and move them into the Love Vibration. Bring them all into Unity Consciousness and remember that we are ALL OF CREATION and that's how we stay in the frequency of Love.

About the Author

Dianne Robbins is a student of the Ascended Master Teachings through the Greatest University of Life, the I AM University of the Radiant Rose Academy.

The Radiant Rose Academy is the Earthly Instrument for this New Dispensation through which the continuation of Progressive Revelation can reach the people of Earth. This is the Dispensation bringing the Divine Feminine back to Earth through Mother Akasha's Rose Pink Rays and Flames of Divine Love, Will and Grace from the Heart of the Great Central Sun.

These are the same Ascended Master Teachings that were taught to Jesus, that prepared him for his Resurrection and Ascension.

Recommended Reading for those on the Ascension Path: Saint Germain's books by Godfre Ray King: *The Magic Presence* and *Unveiled Mysteries*. St. Germain Press, 800.662.2800

Radiant Rose Academy
Vancouver, Canada 604.267.0985
www.akashaonline.com

Made in the USA
San Bernardino, CA
19 August 2016